Learn Xhosa

with
Anne Munnik

Illustrations by Tony Grogan

Shuter & Shooter

PIETERMARITZBURG • CAPE TOWN • RANDBURG • KING WILLIAM'S TOWN

For
My husband and sons

Isinikezelo
Kumyeni wam noonyana bam, uLindile noNono

Book and cover design by Catherine Crookes
Edited by Mary Duncan
Layout by Martingraphix

IT IS ILLEGAL TO PHOTOCOPY ANY PAGES FROM THIS BOOK WITHOUT THE WRITTEN PERMISSION OF THE COPYRIGHT HOLDER

Shuter & Shooter Publishers (Pty) Ltd
Shuters House,
110 CB Downes Road, Pietermaritzburg 3201, KwaZulu-Natal, South Africa
P O Box 61, Mkondeni 3212, KwaZulu-Natal, South Africa
http//:www.shuters.com

Copyright © Shuter & Shooter Publishers (Pty) Ltd 2006

First edition 1994
Second edition 1995
Third edition 1996
Revised edition 2004
Fourth edition 2006
Fifth impression 2012
Sixth impression 2013

ISBN 978 07960 2672 9

Printed by Intrepid Printers (Pty) Ltd, Pietermaritzburg, KwaZulu-Natal
9608

Preface

When Nelson Mandela became South Africa's first democratically elected president on 10 May 1994, he urged the people of South Africa to learn each others' languages. This, he said, would be "the best way to contribute to nation building and reconciliation".

It is never too late to learn!

It is not only a sign of respect to learn another's language but it can also be a rewarding experience, opening up a whole new world.

Xhosa is not easy to learn. It is totally different from the structure of European languages and there is no fundamental connection in the vocabulary as between English and Afrikaans. This book is a simple introduction to the Xhosa language, with intermittent snippets of information about the people and their culture.

The content of the book is manageable, allowing you to work through the exercises at your own pace, with or without assistance.

It goes without saying that progress is directly related to effort! To those who are about to embark on this learning adventure ......
Qhubelani phambili bafundi! – Drive/press forwards students!

Anne Munnik
October 1994

Note to 4th edition

Twelve years have passed since *Learn Xhosa with Anne Munnik* was first published in 1994. Since then we have seen a new South Africa and the development of our Rainbow Nation. We have come a long way, and so has this book.

We revamped *Learn Xhosa* for the fourth edition, with a fresh and contemporary look. For this, the fourth edition, there have been some futher refinements and a few additions. For any author, the success of a book lies in the value it holds for the reader. The response from students, and teachers, has been most encouraging. It was originally intended for extra-mural classes, and to see it being used in schools, colleges and universities, has been very rewarding.

Let us always be mindful of the Xhosa saying:
Umntu ngumntu ngabantu – A person is a person through (other) people.
By learning one another's languages, in our multi-lingual, multi-cultural society, we learn about each other. This is the true spirit of *Masakhane* – Let us build together.

Through all the years of teaching Xhosa, I have got to know many wonderful people of all ages. I have seen lives enriched and attitudes change as a result of this phenomenon called language. I believe passionately "when you learn a new language, you gain a new soul!"

Makube njalo nakuwe! – May you do likewise!

Anne Munnik
January 2006

"Excuse me, Sir. Mhlangeni wants to know if you'll explain it in Xhosa."

The Author

Anne Brown Munnik grew up on the historic farm Glen Avon near Somerset East in the Eastern Cape where she learnt to speak Xhosa as a child.

She included Xhosa as part of her teaching degree at UCT, along with English and Afrikaans, and later pioneered the first Senior Certificate Xhosa class in Cape Town, at SACS in 1978.

In the 1980s she and her husband spent two years in Italy where, amongst other things, she learnt to speak Italian and coached schoolboy rugby! She has also studied German at the University of Munich in Germany.

For the past 20 years she has been offering Xhosa courses in the corporate sector and has travelled to Ghana, Europe and the United States furthering her language teaching skills.

Anne lives in Cape Town with her husband Peter, and twin sons, Oliver and Simon.

"That's a good start. I asked him what it would cost to send a registered, insured parcel express mail to the Eastern Cape, and he said, 'Molo'."

Contents

Notes

Introduction

Distribution and written form of the Xhosa language

The African or Bantu languages of South Africa can be divided into two main groups: the NGUNI languages and the SOTHO languages.

Xhosa belongs to the **Nguni** group of languages which includes Zulu, Swati and Ndebele. It is the main African language spoken in the Eastern and Western Cape, but is also spoken and understood in other parts of the country. Zulu and Xhosa are the most widely spoken African languages in South Africa.

Xhosa was a spoken language only, rich in oral tradition. Attempts to render the language in **written** form started in about 1820 for missionary and schooling purposes in the Eastern Cape. The Xhosa Bible translation was completed in about 1857 by missionaries with the aid of Tiyo Soga, the great Xhosa essayist and churchman.

The Roman alphabet was used for the writing of Xhosa. However, Xhosa has a great variety of sounds, many of which are not found in English or Afrikaans. Most notable are the **clicks**, which originate from the Khoisan (a commonly used term to denote people formerly known as 'Hottentot' and 'Bushmen'). It was found that the letter **k** could substitute for **c, q**, and **x**.

c	cold	**k**old
q	**q**uick	**k**wick
x	a**x**e	a**ks**

These letters became free to represent the three basic clicks.

The written form of the language will be explored further under the section on Pronunciation.

There are 11 official languages in South Africa:

9 African or Bantu languages, English and Afrikaans.

The nine official African languages are

Xhosa

Zulu

Ndebele   } Nguni languages

Swati

Tswana

N. Sotho (Pedi)   } Sotho languages

Sotho

Tsonga (Shangaan)   Nguni related

Venda

ORIGIN OF THE WORD 'XHOSA'

The Xhosa people today think of themselves as being the common descendants of a great hero named **Xhosa** who lived many hundreds of years ago. Some writers go so far as to assert that Xhosa was the son of Mnguni and the brother of Zulu and Swazi. Such ideas are, at the very least, highly suspect. There is every reason to believe that the word 'Xhosa' is derived from the Khoi 'kosa', meaning 'angry men'. It is not unusual for a people to adopt names invented by outsiders. The belief that all culturally related peoples belong to a single genealogy derives more from the understandable wish to bring order into history than it does from history itself.

The House of Phalo by JB Peires

Vocabulary

In this book, words are grouped into three categories:

Nouns

Verbs

General (all words other than nouns and verbs)

New vocabulary is given at the end of each chapter. Turn to the vocabulary and familiarise yourself with the new words, **before** starting the chapter.

NOUNS
All nouns in Xhosa are divided into **15 classes** or **groups**, according to the prefix.

umfundi (student)	**Class 1**	**Singular**
abafundi (students)	**Class 2**	**Plural**

The **prefix** gives the noun its class.   **um-**   (Class 1)
The **stem** gives the noun its meaning.   **-fundi** (student)

The noun dominates the sentence, and other words in the sentence must agree with the noun. Thus there is a **linking** of words. It is very important to know these classes or groups – the sooner the better.

Note the following Xhosa nouns which have become part of South African English.
She is a **fundi** on birds.   (an expert)
The lamb fell into a **donga**.   (a gully)
That's his **indaba**.   (matter, affair)

Noun classes will only be indicated in the book once those classes have been dealt with.

VERBS
All verbs are introduced in their basic form – the infinitive.

ukuhamba   **to** go

This form always ends in **-a**. (There are only three exceptions)

It is the **stem** of the verb which gives the meaning: **-hamba** (go)

In Xhosa, small segments of language are attached to the verb which alter the meaning of the basic form.

Ndi**sa**funda   I am **still** studying
Ndi**nga**hamba?   **May** I go?
Notice that these sentences consist of *one* word in Xhosa and several in English.

GENERAL
This category contains all the words other than nouns and verbs.

NB

In order to find a noun or verb in the **dictionary**, look under the **stem** of the word.

Nouns	um**ntu**	(person)	
	aba**ntu**	(people)	Look under **-ntu**

Verbs	uku**hamba**	(to **go**)	Look under **-hamba**
	ukw**enza**	(to **do**)	Look under **-enza**

General	**m**olo	(hullo)	
	ewe	(yes)	Look under the first letter
	hayi	(no)	

A limited vocabulary is given in this book. Try to expand it whenever possible.

Grammar

Unless Xhosa is learnt naturally among Xhosa speakers, the learning of fundamental grammar is essential. Without it, one cannot understand the structure of the language, which is totally different from English and Afrikaans. Although complex, the grammar is logical and ordered.

As this is an **introduction** to Xhosa, only the basic grammatical constructions are dealt with. Exceptions are kept to a minimum.

Tape/CD (shaded blocks)

The tape/CD which accompanies this book is intended to help the student develop an ear for both **listening** and **speaking** Xhosa. To begin with, it should be used alongside the book, but later it can be used at any convenient moment.

A few pointers to the student

- Try not to run before you can walk! Be patient, as you gradually acquire more vocabulary and skills.
- Concentrate on **quality** and not quantity to begin with. Rather know how to say a few basic pleasantries than attempt too much and be unsure of yourself.
- Remember to **listen** to the speaker. A great deal can be learnt this way.
- Avoid translating directly from English or Afrikaans into Xhosa. Rather try to get a **feel** for the language.
- Work consistently, especially in the beginning, to build a solid foundation.
- Learn the vocabulary well and try to use your Xhosa at every opportunity. The greater the effort the greater the reward!

Pronunciation

Vowels

It is important to get the correct vowel sounds in Xhosa from the start.
Listed below is an example of each sound for you to learn.

a	as in	**ah**	**a**bantu	(people)
e		**e**gg	il**e**ta	(letter)
i		**i**nk	**i**ntombi	(girl)
o		**o**r	is**o**nka	(bread)
u		**oo**mph	**u**mntu	(person)

Clicks

There are three basic clicks in Xhosa.

c	The sound made to express pity (tut tut).	Tongue in the **front**.
q	The sound made by a cork popping.	Tongue in the **middle**
x	The sound made to get a horse to go faster.	**Sideways** click.

Examples

i**c**i**c**i	(earring)
i**c**awa	(church)
-**c**ela	(ask for)
i**q**anda	(egg)
i**q**a**q**a	(skunk)
-**q**ala	(begin)
i**x**esha	(time)
u**x**olo	(peace)
-**x**o**x**a	(discuss)

NOTE

- The three basic clicks are sufficient to begin with. However, there are variations.
- The **q** is not always followed by a **u** as in English.
- Do not avoid the clicks! Learn one example of each and practise them until you feel confident. Make a point of pronouncing every click you come across properly.

Try the following tongue-twister which makes good use of the **q** click.

Iqaqa liziqikaqika kuqaqaqa lide liqhawuke uqhoqhoqho!   The skunk rolls itself in the couch grass until it breaks (its) windpipe!

There are a number of versions of this tongue-twister, one of which appears in the *Guinness Book of Records* as 'The most difficult tongue-twister in the world.'

Do not feel inadequate if you cannot get your tongue around this one!

Consonants

Basically, Xhosa is a phonetic language, that is, the letters correspond to the sounds.

-hamba	(go)
indoda	(man)
ngoku	(now)

Some consonants are aspirated (consonant + h)

-**bh**ala	(write)	compare	-**b**ala	(count)
-**kh**aba	(kick)		i**k**ati	(cat)
-**ph**eka	(cook)		i**p**eki	(pick)
-**th**atha	(take)		u**t**ata	(father)

NOTE

- -**ph**ila (be well, alive)   The **ph** is not pronounced as **f**!
- isi**f**o (disease)   **f** sound
  isi**ph**o (gift)   **p** sound (aspirated)

It would clearly be unwise to confuse the above!
Sipho is a popular masculine name, meaning **gift**. The feminine is **Siphokazi**.

Combination of consonants (as in English)

ng	as in	linger	**ng**omso	(tomorrow)
ny	as in	Kenya	in**y**ama	(meat)
ts	as in	its	-**ts**ala	(pull)
tsh	as in	cheese	-**tsh**a	(burn)

Combination of consonants (not found in English)

dl	-**dl**ala	(play)	
hl	-**hl**ala	(sit, stay, live)	
ty	-**ty**a	(eat)	
rh	ugqi**rh**a	(doctor)	As in the Afrikaans word '**g**oed'
ndl	i**ndl**u	(house)	
ntl	i**ntl**anzi	(fish)	

NOTE

- There is no **s** in front of **hl** !
  kaku**hl**e (well)
  hlala phantsi (sit down)
  Um**hl**anga
  Hluhluwe Game Reserve (**e** as in **e**gg)

- Notice the difference between:

s	(soft)	enko**s**i (thank you)
z	(hard)	ingo**z**i (danger)

Three final points

1. The accent in Xhosa is generally on the second-last syllable in the word.
   u**ma**ma   (mother)
   -se**ben**za   (work)
   -**the**tha   (talk)
   Thus, if the word has only two syllables or sounds, the accent is on the first.
   inja   (dog)
   iti   (tea)
   yiza!   (come)

2. In Xhosa, two vowels do not normally stand together. There are two exceptions:
   - The prefix of **Class 2a**   oogqirha (doctors)   **oo-**   (as in **awe**)
   - The prefix of **Class 10**   iintombi (girls)   **ii-**   (as in **eel**)

   If two vowels do come together in the formation of a word, then certain changes take place.

3. When speaking, words are often shortened or run together:

enkosi	enkos'	(thanks)
umfana	umfan'	(young man)
kulungile	'lungil'	(it is right/good)
yiza apha	yiz' apha	(come here)

1 Greetings •
Noun Classes 1 & 2 and 1a & 2a

1. Greetings

Molo	used to greet one person
Molweni	used to greet more than one person

Molo/molweni (hullo) may be used as a greeting at any time of the day or night. Remember that the accent is on the second last syllable.

Thus **Mo**lo!

Mol**we**ni!

Molweni!

Molo!

Singular greetings

Molo Themba	Hullo Themba
Molo Nomsa	Hullo Nomsa
Molo tata	Hullo father
Molo mama	Hullo mother
Molo mntwana	Hullo child

Plural greetings

Molweni Themba	Hullo Themba and others
Molweni Nomsa	Hullo Nomsa and others
Molweni tata	Hullo father and others
Molweni mama	Hullo mother and others
Molweni bantwana	Hullo children

NOTE

Ubawo (father) indicates respect, whereas **utata** (dad) shows affection.

FORMS OF ADDRESS

Greetings in Xhosa depend largely on age and familiarity. Younger people are expected to show respect to older people and should address them accordingly. Someone roughly the same age as one's mother is addressed as **mama**, likewise with **tata**. A much older person would be addressed as **makhulu** or **tatomkhulu**. **Sisi** and **bhuti** are generally used for people of one's own age or older, but sometimes even for a young girl and boy. Older people address young people as their children or grandchildren.

Family life is very important in the Xhosa community. Terms expressing family relationships are thus significant. There are different words for **my** father, **your** father and **his/her** father. This also applies to mother, grandfather and grandmother. The other kinship terms are also rich in variation.

2. Noun Classes 1 & 2 and 1a & 2a

Xhosa nouns are divided into several groups or classes according to the prefix.

Nouns consist of two parts: prefix + stem

Class 1	um- + -fundi	umfundi	(student)
Class 2	aba- + -fundi	abafundi	(students)

NOTE

The **prefix** indicates the **class** of the noun.

The **stem** gives the **meaning** of the noun.

Classes 1 & 2 (people only)

Prefixes: um- & aba-

Class 1 (singular)	Class 2 (plural)	
umfundi	**aba**fundi	student
umntu	**aba**ntu	person
umntwana	**aba**ntwana	child
umfazi	**aba**fazi	woman
umfana	**aba**fana	young man

umfundi

Classes 1a & 2a
(personal names, family relations, certain special nouns)

Prefixes: u- & oo-

Class 1a (singular)	Class 2a (plural)	
uThemba	**oo**Themba	Themba (male)
uNomsa	**oo**Nomsa	Nomsa (female)
utata/**u**bawo	**oo**tata/**oo**bawo	father
umama	**oo**mama	mother
utatomkhulu	**oo**tatomkhulu	grandfather
umakhulu	**oo**makhulu	grandmother
ubhuti	**oo**bhuti	brother
usisi	**oo**sisi	sister
ugqi<u>r</u>ha	**oo**gqi<u>r</u>ha	doctor
uThixo	_	God
uQamata	_	Supreme Being

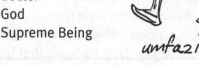

umfazi

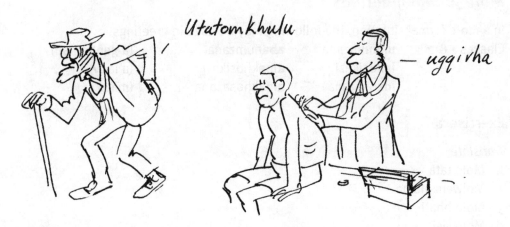

NOTE

- The initial vowel of the noun is always dropped when addressing someone **directly,** as in a greeting.

  uThemba   Molo Themba!

  ooThemba   Molweni Themba!

- **Molweni** indicates that one is greeting, for example, Themba and at least one other. One normally addresses the most senior person in the group, the person best known to one, or the person to whom one is most attached.

- The Class 2a prefix **oo**- is pronounced as in the English **awe**.

  Oobhuti, for example, can mean either brothers or brother and others.

- It is impolite to address a woman as **mfazi**.

Exercise 1

Translate

1. Molo mntwana
2. Molweni bantwana
3. Molo mfundi
4. Molweni bafundi
5. Molweni Nomsa
6. Molo makhulu
7. Molo tatomkhulu
8. Molo mfana
9. Molweni bafana
10. Molo gqirha

More formal greetings

In a more formal situation, the following may be used in greetings.

Classes 1 & 2	**um**numzana	**aba**numzana	(a gentleman)
–	**in**kosikazi	**ama**k̲hosikazi	(a lady)
–	**in**kosazana	**ama**k̲hosazana	(miss)

Exercise 2

Translate

1. Molo tata
2. Molweni mama
3. Molo bhuti
4. Molo sisi
5. Molweni bafundi
6. Molo mnumzana
7. Molo nkosikazi
8. Molo nkosazana
9. Molweni banumzana
10. Molweni makhosikazi

NOTE

- *Umnumzana*, *inkosikazi* and *inkosazana* correspond well to the Afrikaans meneer, mevrou and mejuffrou. Thus:

Molo mnumzana!	When greeting a man
Molweni banumzana!	When greeting more than one man
Molo nkosikazi!	When greeting a woman
Molweni makhosikazi!	When greeting more than one woman
Molo nkosazana!	Hullo miss!
Molweni makhosazana!	Hullo misses!

- Notice how words are often contracted when spoken. **Inkosikazi** can sound like **koskas**!

Saying goodbye

There is in fact no word for 'goodbye'. The expressions 'go well' and 'stay well' are used.

Singular (when speaking to one person only)

Hamba kakuhle!	Go well
Sala kakuhle!	Stay well

Plural (when speaking to more than one person)

Hamba**ni** kakuhle!	Go well
Sala**ni** kakuhle!	Stay well

Exercise 3

Say *'goodbye'* to the following people who are
leaving
1. Go well Themba
2. Go well 'lady'
3. Go well 'mister'
4. Go well children
5. Go well Nomsa and friends
staying
1. Stay well mother
2. Stay well brother
3. Stay well father and friends
4. Stay well ladies
5. Stay well gentlemen

Hamba kakuhle!   Sala kakuhle!

Exercise 4

Greet the following people in Xhosa
1. Someone your mother's age
2. Someone your father's age
3. A child
4. A group of children
5. A lady/woman
6. A group of ladies/women
7. A man
8. A group of men
9. Nomsa (who is leaving)
10. Themba and friends (who are staying)

INCOKO • CONVERSATION

Kunjani?   How are things?
Listen to this little conversation and practise it with a friend.

UThemba:	Molo sisi!
UNomsa:	Molo bhuti!
UThemba:	**Kunjani?**
UNomsa:	**Kulungile/Sikhona**, enkosi. Kunjani kuwe?
UThemba:	Kulungile/Sikhona, enkosi.
UNomsa:	Hamba kakuhle!
UThemba:	Sala kakuhle!

N O T E

- **Kulungile** or **sikhona** may be used. There are several alternatives (see page 16).
- Notice the use of **si-** (we) even when referring to one person. This indicates that one is including one's family and friends. **Ndi**khona may also be used.

ISIGAMA • VOCABULARY

Nouns

Classes

1 & 2	**um**fundi	student
	umntu	person
	umntwana	child
	umfazi	woman
	umfana	young man
	umnumzana	gentleman
1a & 2a	**u**Themba	Themba (m)
	uNomsa	Nomsa (f)
	utata/**u**bawo	father
	umama	mother
	umakhulu	grandmother
	utatomkhulu	grandfather
	ubhuti	brother
	usisi	sister
	ugqirha	doctor
	uThixo	God
	uQamata	Supreme Being
	inkosikazi	lady
	inkosazana	miss
	incoko	conversation
	isigama	vocabulary

Kunjani?   *Kulungile enkosi!*

Verbs

-hamba	go, walk, travel
-sala	stay, remain

General

molo/molweni	hullo (sg & pl)
kakuhle	well
kunjani?	how **is** it?
kulungile	**it is** fine
sikhona	**we**/I am fine
enkosi	thank you
kuwe	**with** you

Verbs (Present Tense) • Pronouns

1. Verbs

Study the following verbs

-bona	see
-funa	want, need, look for
-funda	study, learn, read
-thetha	talk, speak
-thanda	like, love

NOTE

* Verbs are listed under their stems.
* Verb stems end in -**a**.
* The basic form of the verb is the infinitive.
  ukufunda   **to** study or study**ing**.

2. Pronouns (singular)

ndi-	I
u-	you

These are not separate words which can stand on their own, as in English. They are always attached to the verb. They are the equivalent of the English pronoun.

Ndibona uNomsa	**I** see Nomsa
Ndifunda isiXhosa	**I** study Xhosa
Uthetha kakuhle	**You** speak well
Uthanda ukufunda	**You** like studying

The present tense

In English there are several ways of expressing the present tense. This is not the case in Xhosa. Right from the start, aim towards developing a feel for the language, instead of trying to translate literally.

Ndifunda isiXhosa   I study Xhosa
                                  I do study Xhosa
                                  I am studying Xhosa

Study the following examples

Ndiyabona	I see
Ndibona uNomsa	I see Nomsa
Ndiyafunda	I study
Ndifunda isiXhosa	I study Xhosa
Uyathetha	You speak
Uthetha isiNgesi	You speak English

N o t e

In the above sentences it is clear that **-ya-** is placed before the verb stem if there is no word following the verb. The **-ya-** has no meaning and occurs only in the **present tense positive.** It is a peculiarity of the language for which there is no English or Afrikaans equivalent.

Exercise 1

Translate into English
1. Ndiyahamba
2. Uyasala
3. Ndifuna ukuhamba
4. Ufuna ukusala
5. Ndithanda uNomsa
6. Uyafunda
7. Ndiyabona
8. Uthetha isiAfrikansi
9. Ndifuna ugqirha
10. Ndithanda ukufunda isiXhosa

Exercise 2

Translate into Xhosa
1. I am studying
2. I am studying Xhosa
3. I like to speak Xhosa
4. You are going
5. You want to go

Pronouns (plural)

si-	we
ni-	you

As with **ndi-** and **u-**, **si-** and **ni-** are always attached to the verb.

Siyafunda	**We** are learning
Sifunda isiXhosa	**We** are learning Xhosa
Niyathetha	**You** are speaking
Nithetha isiNgesi	**You** are speaking English

Exercise 3

Translate into Xhosa

1. I am looking for a doctor
2. We need water
3. You (sg) like tea
4. You (pl) like coffee
5. We are going
6. I am well/in good health
7. We are well/in good health
8. I am learning to speak Xhosa
9. We are learning to speak Xhosa
10. You speak well (sg and pl)

Molweni bantwana! Ninjani?

Molo Mama! Siyaphila.

NOTE

kakuhle	well, nicely
-phila	be well or in good health

INCOKO • CONVERSATION

Molweni bantwana!   *Hullo children!*

Umama:	Molweni bantwana!
Abantwana:	Molo mama!
Umama:	**Ni**njani?
Abantwana:	**Si**yaphila. Kunjani kuwe?
Umama:	Ndiyaphila, enkosi.
Abantwana:	Sala kakuhle mama!
Umama:	Hambani kakuhle bantwana!

INGOMA • SONG

Molweni nonke!	Hullo everyone
Niphila njani?	How are **you**?
Sisaphil' enkosi!	**We** are *still* fine thank you!
Kunjani ku**we**?	How is it with **you**?

ISIGAMA • VOCABULARY

Nouns

isiXhosa	Xhosa
isiNgesi	English
isiAfrikansi	Afrikaans
amanzi	water
iti	tea
ikofu	coffee
ingoma	song

Verbs

-bona	see
-funa	want, need, look for
-funda	study, learn, read
-thetha	speak, talk
-thanda	like, love
-phila	be well/in good health

General

ndi-	I
u-	you (singular)
si-	we
ni-	you (plural)
uku-	**to** + verb stem
njani?	how?
nonke	everyone/all of **you**
-sa-	still

3

ЇЇЇЇЇЇЇЇ **Questions**

INCOKO • CONVERSATION
Uphila njani? How are you?

UJohn:	Molo Sipho!
USipho:	Molo John!
UJohn:	**Uphila njani?**
USipho:	**Ndiphila kakuhle.** Wena uphila njani?
UJohn:	Hayi, **ndisaphila,** enkosi.
USipho:	Uvela phi?
UJohn:	Ndivela **e**khaya.
USipho:	Uya phi ngoku?
UJohn:	Ndiya **e**msebenz**ini.** / Ndiya **e**sikol**weni.**
USipho:	Uyasebenza namhlanje? / Uyafunda namhlanje?
UJohn:	Ewe, ndiyasebenza. / Ewe, ndiyafunda.
USipho:	Oo... ndiyabona. Hamba kakuhle John!
UJohn:	Sala kakuhle Sipho!

NOTE

- **Hayi**, ndisaphila   **No**, I am still fine.
  Hayi is often used in this way. (As in the Afrikaans, **nee goed**)

- Uya**sebenza** namhlanje?   Are you **working** today?
  The -ya- is retained here because the emphasis is on the *verb* and not on the word following. Compare:
  Usebenza **namhlanje**?   Are you working **today**?
  Thus, if the word following the verb is *not* a noun, the -ya- may or may not be used, depending on the emphasis.

Isigama

wena	as for you
hayi	no
phi?	where?
ekhaya	**from** home
ngoku	now
namhlanje	today
ewe	yes
-vela	come **from**
-ya	go **to**
-sebenza	work (verb)

NOTE

- **uku**sebenza   **to** work (verb)
  umsebenz**i**   work, job (noun)
  emsebenz**ini**   **to/from/at** work

- **uku**funda   **to** study (verb)
  isikolo   school (noun)
  esikol**weni**   **to/from/at** school

INCOKO • CONVERSATION

Ngubani igama lakho?   *What is your name?*

UThemba:	Molo sisi!
UNomsa:	Molo bhuti!
UThemba:	**Ngubani igama lakho?**
UNomsa:	**NguNomsa igama lam.** Ngubani igama lakho?
UThemba:	NguThemba igama lam.
UNomsa:	**Ndiyavuya uku<u>kw</u>azi** Themba.
UThemba:	**Nam, ndiyavuya uku<u>kw</u>azi** Nomsa.
UNomsa:	Uhlala phi?
UThemba:	Ndihlala eGugulethu. Wena, uhlala phi?
UNomsa:	Ndihlala eRondebosch.
UThemba:	Uyagoduka ngoku?
UNomsa:	Ewe, ndiyagoduka.
UThemba:	Hamba kakuhle Nomsa!
UNomsa:	Sala kakuhle Themba!

Ngubani igama lakho?

NguNomsa igama lam

NOTE

- **Ng**ubani igama lakho?
  NguJohn igama lam   *or*
  Igama lam **ng**uJohn

  What **is** your name?
  My name **is** John.

- Ndiyavuya uku<u>kw</u>azi

  I am glad to know <u>you</u>   *or*
  I am pleased to meet <u>you</u>.

  Nam ndiyavuya uku<u>kw</u>azi

  I too am pleased to meet <u>you</u>.

Isigama

igama **lam**	**my** name
igama **lakho**	**your** name
nam	I, too
eGugulethu	**in** Gugulethu
eRondebosch	**in** Rondebosch
ngoku	now
-vuya	be glad
-azi	know
-hlala	live
-goduka	go-home
Compare:	**-hlala** (live, stay)
	-sala (remain, stay behind)

After going through the chapter, try to learn these two conversations by heart. You will find that it is a great booster to have everyday situations like these at your fingertips.

Questions

As you may have noticed there are two types of questions in Xhosa, those which contain a 'question word' or interrogative, and those which do not.

Questions which *do not* contain a 'question word'

Uyaphila?	Are you well?
Uyahamba?	Are you going?
Ufuna iti?	Do you want tea?
Niyafunda?	Are you (pl) studying?
Nifunda isiXhosa?	Are you (pl) studying Xhosa?

NOTE

* **Uyahamba**   You are going

   Uyahamba?   Are you going?

   The statement and the question look alike, except for the question mark. However, when speaking, the voice is raised for a question. Sometimes **na** is added to the end of a question to make the distinction quite clear. It has no meaning.

   Uyahamba **na?**   Are you going?

* Uyafunda?   **Are** you studying / **Do** you study?

* To this type of question (one without a 'question word') one answers **yes** or **no**.
   Uyafunda?   **Ewe**, ndiyafunda or
                        Hayi, ndiyasebenza

NB At this stage, one can only answer 'no' in the above way!

Complete the answers to the following questions

1. Uyasebenza?   Ewe, ...
2. Uyahamba?   Hayi, ...
3. Ufunda isiXhosa?   Ewe, ...
4. Nifuna iti?   Hayi, ...
5. Niyaphila?   Ewe, ...

NOTE

- The verb **-phila** means **live, be alive**, but has the general meaning of **being in good health**. There are many ways of asking after someone's health.

  Uyaphila?   Are you healthy/well?
  Usaphila?   Are you **still** well?
  Uphila kakuhle?   Are you (living) well?
  Uphila **njani**?   **How** are you?
  Uphilile?   Are you well? is a popular version.

- **-ya-** and **-sa-** are never used together.

Exercise 2

Translate the following questions and answers into Xhosa

1. Do you understand?   Yes, I understand
2. Do you live at home?   Yes, I live at home
3. Do you (pl) want water?   Yes, we want water
4. Are you sick?   Yes, I am sick
5. Are you working?   No, I am still studying
6. Are you (pl) going home **today**? Yes, we are going home today
7. Are you well?   No, I am sick
8. Are you (pl) **going** now?   Yes, we are going now
9. Are you glad?   Yes, I am glad
10. Do you speak Xhosa?   Yes, I speak a little

Questions which *do* contain a 'question word'

Uphila **njani?**	**How** are you?
Uvela **phi?**	**Where** do you come from?
Ufuna **ntoni?**	**What** do you want?
Ufuna **bani?**	**Whom** do you want?
Uhamba **nini?**	**When** are you going?

NOTE

- The 'question word' comes **after** the verb.

- -ya- is **never** used in a sentence with a 'question word'

- One cannot answer **yes** or **no** to this type of question!

Question words

njani?	how?
phi?	where?
ntoni?	what?
bani?	who/whom?
nini?	when?

Learn these well!

Exercise 3

Answer the following questions in Xhosa

1. Uphila njani?
2. Uvela phi?
3. Ufuna ntoni?
4. Ufuna bani?
5. Uhamba nini?
6. Niphila njani?
7. Niya phi?
8. Nifunda ntoni?
9. Nibona bani?
10. Nihamba nini?

NOTE

- There are a number of ways of expressing **why**:
  - **Kutheni?**
  - **Ngokuba?/Ngoba?**

  These function differently from the other question words. At this stage, merely recognise them and use them on their own to ask 'why'.

- Uthi**ni?**   **What** do you say? What's up/what's happening?
  Ufuna**ni?**   **What** do you want?
  Ntoni may be shortened to **-ni** and added to the verb as above.

Fill in the correct question word

1. Ufunda .... ?   Ndifunda isiXhosa
2. Nivela .... ?   Sivela eKapa
3. Ufuna .... ?   Ndifuna uLizo
4. Niphila .... ?   Siphilile enkosi
5. Ubona .... ?   Ndibona imoto
6. Uya .... ?   Ndiya eGoli
7. Ubona .... ?   Ndibona abantwana
8. Nifuna .... ?   Sifuna umsebenzi
9. Ugoduka .... ?   Ndigoduka namhlanje
10. Uhamba .... ?   Ndihamba ngoku

NOTE

- **-vela** (come from) has two meanings: **Uvela phi?**
  1. Where do you come (hail) from?   Ndivela **eBhayi**
  2. Where have you (just) come from?   Ndivela **ekhaya**

- **-hlala** (live/stay, sit) has two meanings:
  1. *I live/stay* in Khayelitsha   Ndi**hlala** eKhayelitsha
  2. Do you want *to sit* down?   Ufuna uku**hlala** phantsi?

- -hamba   go, walk, travel (no destination mentioned)
  -ya   **go TO** ... (always a **destination** mentioned)
  -goduka   go home
  Ndiyahamba   I am going
  Ndi**ya** eMonti   I am **going TO** East London
  Ndiyagoduka   I am going home

NB There is no connection between -ya- and the verb uku**ya** (to **go TO** ....)

Various ways of asking *'How are you?'* (Using *njani?*)

Kunjani?	How is **it**?
Unjani?	How are **you**? (sg)
Ninjani?	How are **you**? (pl)
Uphila njani?	How are **you** (sg) in health?
Niphila njani?	How are **you** (pl) in health?

To these questions, replies are also varied.

Kulungile	**It is** good/alright
Ndi**sa**phila	I am **still** healthy/well
Siphil**ile**	We are healthy/well
Ndiphila **kakuhle**	I am (living) **well**
Sikhona	**We** are well (lit. we are there!)

Summary

> **There are two types of questions:**
> - **No 'question word'** (Answer **yes** or **no**)
>
> | | |
> |---|---|
> | Uyafunda? | Are you studying? |
> | Ufunda **isiXhosa**? | Are you studying **Xhosa**? |
>
> - **With a 'question word'** (Cannot answer yes or no)
>
> | | |
> |---|---|
> | Ufunda **ntoni?** | **What** are you studying? |
> | Ufuna **bani?** | **Whom** do you want? |
> | Uphila **njani?** | **How** are you? |
> | Uvela **phi?** | **Where** do you come from? |
> | Uhamba **nini?** | **When** are you going? |

GREETINGS

Greetings are an integral part of African life. It is then customary to enquire after someone's health and that of their family. In Xhosa, even though one person is speaking or being spoken to, the plural form is often used.

Ninjani?	How are you (and your family)?
Siphilile	I am well (and my family)

There are clearly many ways of enquiring after someone's health and of responding. To begin with, choose one 'question and answer' with which you feel happy, and use this with confidence. For example: **Kunjani?**

Sikhona

However, see that you are familiar with the other variations, so that you can recognise them in conversation and respond appropriately.

Two exceptions

- What is your name/surname?

  1. | | |
      |---|---|
      | **Ngubani** igama lakho? | **What is** your name? |
      | **Ngu**Themba (igama lam) | **It is** Themba (my name) |

      or

Ungubani?	Who **are you**? (lit. you are who?)
NdinguThemba	**I am** Themba

  2. | | |
      |---|---|
      | **Ngubani** ifani yakho? | **What is** your surname? |
      | **Ngu**Sibeko (ifani yam) | **It is** Sibeko (my surname) |

- **What is the time?**
  Ngubani ixesha?   **What is** the time?
  Ngu 2:30   **It is** 2:30

N O T E

- Clearly in these questions **bani** (who) is used for the English **what**.

- **ng** means **is/am/are** + noun (here **ubani**)
- Numbers in Xhosa are complicated. Most Xhosa speakers are familiar with the English numbers, and in fact use them a great deal. They are a lot simpler!

Exercise 5

Translate into Xhosa

1. What is your name?   It is ....
2. What is your surname?   It is ....
3. Who are you?   I am ....
4. What is the time?   It is ....
5. Where do you come from?   I come from ....
6. Where do you live?   I live in ....
7. Do you work?   Yes, I do work
8. Where do you work?   I work in Cape Town
9. Do you speak English?   No, I speak Xhosa
10. What do you want/need?   I want/need work

INCOKO • CONVERSATION

Uyaphangela?   *Do you work? meaning Do you have a job?*

UKhosi:	Molo!
UJenny:	Molo!
UKhosi:	Kunjani?
UJenny:	Sikhona, enkosi. Kunjani kuwe?
UKhosi:	Hayi, sikhona. **Ungu**bani wena?
UJenny:	**Ndingu**Jenny Brown.
UKhosi:	Oo! Mna **ndingu**Khosi Mlambo.
UJenny:	**Ndiyavuya ukuku̱wazi** Khosi.
UKhosi:	**Nam ndiyavuya ukuku̱wazi** Jenny.

UJenny:	Uhlala phi?
UKhosi:	Ndihlala **e**Sea Point. Wena uhlala phi?
UJenny:	Ndihlala **e**Newlands.
UKhosi:	Uyaphangela?
UJenny:	Hayi, ndisafunda. Wena, uyaphangela?
UKhosi:	Ewe ndisebenza kwaWoolworths.
UJenny:	**Ngu**bani ixesha?
UKhosi:	**Ngu** 5:30.
UJenny:	Yho! Kuleythi. Ndiyagoduka.
UKhosi:	Hamba kakuhle Jenny!
UJenny:	Sala kakuhle Khosi!

NOTE

ukuphangela	to work (to be employed)
ukusebenza	to work (in general)

ISIGAMA • VOCABULARY

Nouns

Class

1a	**u**Sipho	Sipho (m)
	uLizo	Lizo (m)
	uKhosi	Khosi (f)
–	**i**khaya	home
–	**um**sebenzi	work, job
–	**isi**kolo	school
–	**i**gama	name
–	**i**fani	surname
–	**i**xesha	time
–	**i**moto	car

Verbs

-vela	come from
-ya	go **TO**... (destination)
-sebenza	work
-vuya	be glad
*-az**i**	know
-hlala	stay, live, sit
-goduka	go home
-qonda	understand
-gula	be sick
-zama	try
*-th**i**	say
-phangela	work (be employed)
exceptions	*verb stems end in -i*

General

wena	as for you (singular)
hayi	no
ekhaya	**from/at** home
ngoku	now
emsebenz**ini**	**to/at/from** work
esikol**weni**	**to/at/from** school
namhlanje	today
ewe	yes
igama **lam**	**my** name
igama **lakho**	**your** name
nam	I/me too
kancinci	a little
njani?	how?
phi?	where?
ntoni?	what?
bani?	who?
nini?	when?
kutheni? ⎫	why?
ngo(ku)ba? ⎭	
eKapa	**from** Cape Town
eGoli	**to** Johannesburg
eBhayi	**in** Port Elizabeth
eMonti	**at** East London
kulungile	**it is** good/alright/ fine/okay

sikhona	I am/**we** are well
mna	as for me
kwa-	at (the place of)
yho!	gosh!
kuleythi	**it is** late

20

4 Noun Classes 3 & 4, 5 & 6, 7 & 8 • Verb Links (Classes 1 – 8)

1. Noun Classes 3 & 4, 5 & 6, 7 & 8

As mentioned in the introduction, the sooner you get to know the classes, the better. Now that Classes 1 & 2 and 1a & 2a are familiar, Classes 3 & 4, 5 & 6, and 7 & 8 are introduced at the same time, to allow for comparison of these classes. To begin with, try to associate the singular and plural prefixes rather than the numbers, for example the **um-** & **aba-** Classes and **u-** & **oo-** Classes.

Study the following examples
Each noun is in its own class. The class is indicated by the **prefix**.

1. Ndifuna **um**sebenzi   I am looking for **work**
   Sifuna **imi**sebenzi eMzantsi Afrika   We need **jobs** in South Africa
2. Ndifuna **i**qanda   I want an **egg**
   Sifuna **ama**qanda   We want **eggs**
3. Ndifuna ukuthenga **isi**pho   I want to buy a **gift**
   Sifuna ukuthenga **izi**pho   We want to buy **gifts**

Classes 3 & 4

Prefixes: um- &   **imi-**
Class 3 (singular)   **Class 4** (plural)

umsebenzi	**imi**sebenzi	work, job, exercise
umbuzo	**imi**buzo	question
umlilo	**imi**lilo	fire
umoya	**imi**moya	wind
uMzantsi Afrika	–	South Africa

umoya   umlilo

UMzantsi Afrika

Classes 5 & 6

Prefixes: ili-/i- &   ama-
Class 5 (singular)   **Class 6** (plural)

Stems of one syllable or sound

ilifu	**ama**fu	cloud
ilitye	**ama**tye	stone
ilizwe	**ama**zwe	country
ilizwi	**ama**zwi	word
iliso	*****ame**hlo	eye
	*exception	

Stems of more than one syllable or sound

igama	**ama**gama	name
ikhaya	**ama**khaya	home
ixesha	**ama**xesha	time
iqanda	**ama**qanda	egg
icici	**ama**cici	earring
iwele	**ama**wele	twin

iqanda   amaqanda

NOTE

- Nouns of Class 5 take the prefix **ili-** or **i-** depending on whether the stem has one syllable or more. The plural prefix is always **ama-**.
- The above nouns which take the prefix **i-** are **genuine** Xhosa words.
- The following nouns which take the prefix **i-** are **borrowed** from English or Afrikaans:

iphepha	**ama**phepha	paper, page
itikiti	**ama**tikiti	ticket
ivili	**ama**vili	wheel
ipolisa	**ama**polisa	policeman

- The following nouns have no singular:

amanzi	water
amasi	sour milk
amafutha	fat, oil
amandla	power, strength

- Exception: Classes 1 & 6

umXhosa	**ama**Xhosa	a Xhosa
umZulu	**ama**Zulu	a Zulu

Classes 7 & 8

Prefixes: isi- &   **izi-**

Class 7 (singular)   **Class 8** (plural)

isiXhosa	–	Xhosa
isiNgesi	–	English
isiAfrikansi	–	Afrikaans
isiZulu	–	Zulu
isiSuthu	–	Sotho
isigama	–	vocabulary
isifundo	**izi**fundo	lesson
isihlangu	**izi**hlangu	shoe
isipho	**izi**pho	gift
isifo	**izi**fo	disease

isipho

isifo

NOTE

- If the stem begins with a **vowel**, isi- → is-, for example:

  isonka   bread

  isandla/**iz**andla   hand/hands

- Generally, if a **borrowed*** word begins with an **s-** (followed by a consonant) it belongs to Classes 7 & 8.

  isikolo   school

  isitulo   chair

  isitena   brick

  isitalato   street

  isitampu   stamp

  *All the above words, with the exception of 'isitampu', are borrowed from Afrikaans.

- Languages fall into Class 7 and thus prefix **isi-**.

- Both **isiAfrikansi** and **isiBhulu** (derived from 'boer') are used for the Afrikaans language. However, the latter is no longer relevant, given the wide usage of Afrikaans in South Africa today.

Fill in the correct noun and translate

1. Namhlanje kukho .... (wind)
2. Ngubani .... (the time)?
3. Funda .... (the vocabulary) kakuhle!
4. Sihlala .... (**in** South Africa)
5. Niqonda .... (Sotho)?
6. .... (name) lam nguMary
7. Ndithenga .... (tickets) namhlanje
8. Ufuna .... (work)?
9. Sifuna .... (water)
10. Ndifuna ukuthenga .... (a gift)

NOTE

There is no equivalent in Xhosa for **a, an, the**. For instance, **umlilo** can mean **fire, a fire,** or **the fire.**

The English translation will depend on the context in which the noun is used in the sentence.

Summary of Noun Classes 1 - 8

Class	Noun	Prefix	Meaning
1	**um**ntu	**um-**	person
2	**aba**ntu	**aba-**	people
1a	**u**tata	**u-**	father
2a	**oo**tata	**oo-**	father & others
3	**um**sebenzi	**um-**	work, job
4	**imi**sebenzi	**imi-**	jobs
5	**ili**fu : **i**gama	**ili-** or **i-**	cloud : name
6	**ama**fu : **ama**gama	**ama-**	clouds : names
7	**isi**pho	**isi-**	gift
8	**izi**pho	**izi-**	gifts

INGOMA • SONG

Umzi Watsha   *'London' is burning*

Umzi watsha! Umzi watsha!   The homestead is burning!
Khangela phaya! Khangela phaya!   Look over there!
Umlilo! Umlilo!   Fire!
Galel' amanzi! Galel' amanzi!   Pour on water!

UMZI

Traditionally, the head of the household would build his **umzi,** or group of huts, facing east and preferably on a slope to allow for drainage in wet weather. Another important factor was that it should be fairly close to a source of fresh water.

Several **first names** include the word *umzi*. It can have a literal and an idiomatic meaning.

uVus**umzi**   One who wakes up the household (-vusa)
                         One who keeps the family name alive
uMziwakhe   His home
                         He is the heir to his home/family
uMzimkhulu   Big home
                         He is enlarging the *umzi*, by carrying on the family name.

The names of some **rivers** also include the word *umzi*.

uMzimkhulu   The big 'home'
uMzimvubu   The home of the hippopotamus (imvubu)
uMzinyathi   The home of the buffalo (inyathi)

25

2. Verb Links (Classes 1–8)

Classes 1 & 2 and 1a & 2a

Listen to the following passage, read it aloud and translate.

Umsebenzi 2

Abafundi **ba**funda isiXhosa. **Ba**funda kakuhle.
UJohn **u**thi: '**Ndi**thanda ukuthetha isiXhosa'
UMary **u**thi: 'Nam, **ndi**thanda ukuthetha isiXhosa'
OoJohn **ba**thi: '**Si**yafunda! **Si**yavuya!'
UMnumzana Mhlaba, utitshala, uthi: 'Bafundi, nisebenza kamnandi!'

N OTE

- The **Verb Links** here are the equivalent of the English pronoun.
  He and **she** are indicated by **u-**, and **they** by **ba-**.
- Class 1a   **uMnumzana (uMnu)**   Mister (Mr)
  Class 1   **um**numzana   gentleman

The English pronouns are:

	Singular	Plural
1st Person:	I	we
2nd Person:	you	you
3rd Person:	he, she, it	they

The Xhosa equivalent of these pronouns is the **Verb Link**.
The 1st and 2nd persons have already been dealt with.

1st Person:	ndi-	si-
2nd Person:	u-	ni-
3rd Person:	In Xhosa the 3rd person is made up of the **noun classes**.	

Study the following examples

Umfundi **u**yafunda	The student (**he/she**) is studying
UThemba **u**yasebenza	Themba (**he**) is working
Abafundi **ba**yafunda	The students (**they**) are studying
OoThemba **ba**yasebenza	Themba and others (**they**) are working

- From these examples it is clear that the **Verb Link** is derived from the *prefix* of the noun:

  Class 1   **um-**   →   **u-**   (he/she)
  Class 2   **aba-**   →   **ba-**   (they)

  Classes 1a and 2a are subsidiary classes of 1 and 2 and therefore take the same links respectively.

- When a noun is the subject of a sentence, the verb link must nevertheless be used.
  It **links** the noun to the verb.

  Umfazi **u**yagula   The woman (**she**) is sick
  Ugula kakhulu   **She** is very sick

- There is no **gender** in Xhosa.

  Umntwana **u**yagula   The child (**he/she**) is sick
  UThemba **u**yagula   Themba (**he**) is sick
  UNomsa **u**yagula   Nomsa (**she**) is sick

  Thus **u-** represents both **he** and **she**, and the gender will depend on the noun.
  For example, **u**yagula means **he** is sick or **she** is sick.
  This is the reason Xhosa speakers may use **she** for a male, and vice versa.

- The only difference between
  u- meaning you (singular) and
  u- meaning he/she, is in the tone of voice.
  You is said in a lower tone, while **he/she** is said in a higher tone.

N O T E

- Every syllable in a word has a slightly different tone. It is not easy for a non-mother tongue speaker to distinguish between these tones. As you progress, merely try to be aware of them. In some cases, a difference in tone means a difference in meaning. For example, **amathanga** can mean 'thighs' or 'pumpkins', depending on the tone!

The **Verb Link** is derived from the *prefix* of the noun.

Class 1	**um-**	→	**u-**	he/she
Class 2	**aba-**	→	**ba-**	they
Class 1a	*		**u-**	he/she/it
Class 2a	*		**ba-**	they

* Remember: Classes 1a and 2a take the same links as Classes 1 and 2!

Umsebenzi 3

Fill in the correct verb link and translate

a) 1. Umntu ......yathetha
   2. UMary ......thenga izitampu
   3. Umfazi ......yasebenza
   4. Umfundi ......funda isiXhosa
   5. Utata ......ncedisa ubhuti

b) 1. Abantu ......yavuya
   2. OoMeri ......yavuya
   3. Abafazi ......yaphangela
   4. Abafundi ......qonda kakuhle
   5. Ootata ......ncedisa inkosikazi

Umsebenzi 4

Fill in the correct verb link and translate

1. Umntwana ...... yadlala.   ......dlala kamnandi.
2. Abantwana ..... yancedisa.   ......ncedisa abazali.
3. Umakhulu ...... yagula.   ...... gula kakhulu.
4. Oobhuti ...... yahamba.   ......hamba ngoku.
5. ULumkile ...... yasela.   ...... sela iFanta.
6. Abazali ...... yaphunga.   ...... phunga iti.
7. Umfana ...... yatya.   ...... tya isonka.
8. Utitshalakazi ...... yathetha.   ...... thetha ngaphandle.
9. Abanumzana ...... yasebenza   ......sebenza ngaphakathi.
10. Umfazi ...... yathenga.   ...... thenga amaqanda.

NOTE

UThandi uthetha ka**khulu**	Thandi speaks **a lot**
UThandi uthetha ka**ncinci**	Thandi speaks **a little** or **softly**
UThandi uthetha kaku**hle**	Thandi speaks **well**
UThandi uthetha ka**mnandi**	Thandi speaks **nicely** or **pleasantly**

Useful examples

Enkosi **kakhulu**	Thank you **very much**
Ndithetha isiXhosa **kancinci**	I speak a **little** Xhosa
Hamba **kakuhle**!	Go **well**
Abantwana badlala **kamnandi**	The children play **nicely**

Translate into Xhosa
1. The people are going
2. The doctor helps people
3. Father drinks coffee but mother drinks tea
4. The child likes porridge
5. John is reading the newspaper
6. The young men want work
7. Thandi and the others are working
8. The children live at home
9. Sipho lives in Cape Town but Thandi lives in Port Elizabeth
10. We live in South Africa

Classes 3 & 4, 5 & 6, 7 & 8

Study the following examples

1. **Um**oya **u**yavuthuza   The wind (it) is blowing
   Imithetho **i**yatshintsha   The laws (they) are changing
2. **I**xesha **li**yahamba   The time (it) is going (fast)
   Amapolisa **a**ncedisa umfana   The police (they) help the young man
3. **Isi**pho **si**vela <u>ku</u>mama   The gift (it) comes <u>from</u> mother
   Izipho **zi**vela <u>ku</u>mama   The gifts (they) come <u>from</u> mother.

The **Verb Link** is derived from the *prefix* of the noun.

Class 3	**um-**	→	**u-**	it
Class 4	**imi-**	→	**i-**	they
Class 5	**ili- & i-**	→	**li-**	it
Class 6	**ama-**	→	**a-**	they
Class 7	**isi-**	→	**si-**	it
Class 8	**izi-**	→	**zi-**	they

NOTE

- Since most of the nouns in these classes are things and not people, they are largely used as the **object** (the part after the verb).

For example:
Ufuna **umsebenzi**   He wants work
Basela **amanzi**   They are drinking water
Bathetha **isiXhosa**   They are speaking Xhosa

Umsebenzi 6

Complete the following as shown in the example

umlilo   **imi**lilo   3 & 4   fire

1. **um**buzo
2. **isi**tulo
3. **i**vili
4. **um**thetho
5. **isi**fo
6. **ili**zwe
7. **um**thi
8. **i**phephandaba
9. **isi**kolo
10. **um**pu

Umsebenzi 7

Fill in the correct verb link and word. Translate into English

1. Umama ...thenga ....   (bread)
2. UZola ...galela ....   (water)
3. Abantwana ...thanda ukutya ....   (porridge)
4. Umfundi ...buza ....   (a question)
5. OoThemba ...funda ....   (the newspaper)
6. Ipolisa ...buza ....   (questions)
7. Umzali ...funa ....   (a doctor)
8. Umoya ...vuthuza kakhulu ....   (in Cape Town)
9. Umsebenzi ...tshintsha ....
   (the wheel)
10. Amawele ...hleli ....
    (nicely)

Listen to the following passage, read it aloud, and then answer the questions.

UJoseph Mlambo **u**yaphangela. **U**sebenza eKapa. **U**thanda umsebenzi *wakhe* kakhulu. **U**thanda ukuhlala eKapa kodwa **u**thi umoya **u**vuthuza gqitha! Inkosikazi *yakhe*, uLindiwe, **u**hlala ekhaya. Usebenza kakhulu ekhaya. Abantwana **ba**yafunda. **Ba**funda eVuyani, eGugulethu. Ekhaya, **ba**ncedisa abazali kakhulu. OoMlambo **ba**hleli kamnandi!

Umoya uvuthuza gqitha!

Umsebenzi 8

Imibuzo • *Answer the following questions*
1. UMnumzana Mlambo uyaphangela?
2. Usebenza phi?
3. Uthanda umsebenzi wakhe?
4. Umoya unjani eKapa?
5. UNkosikazi Mlambo uyasebenza?
6. Usebenza phi?
7. Abantwana bayafunda?
8. Bafunda phi?
9. Bancedisa bani ekhaya?
10. OoMlambo bahleli njani eKapa?

Isigama

kodwa	but	umsebenzi wa**khe**	**his/her** work
gqitha	a lot, too much	inkosikazi ya**khe**	**his** work
ba**hleli**	they **are living**		
kamnandi	nice**ly**		

NOTE

- **u**Mnumzana Mlambo   Mr Mlambo
  umnumzana   a gentleman
- **u**Nkosikazi Mlambo   Mrs Mlambo
  inkosikazi   a lady, wife
- inkosi   chief (originally of royal blood); lord, ruler, master
  inkosi**kazi**   chief's wife; lady, wife, madam
  inkos**ana**   chief's son; a petty chief, chieftain
  inkos**azana**   chief's daughter; young lady, miss

ISIGAMA

Nouns

Class

3 & 4	**um**sebenzi	work, job, exercise
	umbuzo	question
	umlilo	fire
	umoya	wind, air
	uMzantsi Afrika	South Africa
	umzi	homestead
	umthetho	law
	umthi	tree
	umpu	gun
	umlambo	river
5 & 6	**ili**fu	cloud
	ilitye	stone
	ilizwe	country
	ilizwi	word, voice
	iliso	eye
	igama	name
	ikhaya	home
	ixesha	time
	iqanda	egg
	iwele	twin
	icici	earring
	iphepha	paper, page
	iphephandaba	newspaper
	itikiti	ticket
	ivili	wheel
	ipolisa	policeman

	amanzi	water
	amasi	sour milk
	amafutha	fat, oil
	amandla	power, strength
1 & 6	**um**Xhosa/**ama-**	a Xhosa
	umZulu/**ama-**	a Zulu
7 & 8	**isi**Xhosa	Xhosa
	isiNgesi	English
	isiAfrikansi	Afrikaans
	isiZulu	Zulu
	isiSuthu	Sotho
	isigama	vocabulary
	isifundo	lesson
	isihlangu	shoe
	isipho	gift
	isifo	disease
	isonka	bread
	isandla	hand
	isikolo	school
	isitulo	chair
	isitena	brick
	isitampu	stamp
	isitalato	street
	isidudu	porridge
1 & 2	**um**numzana	gentleman
	umzali	parent
	umsebenzi	worker
1a & 2a	**u**titshala	teacher
	utitshala**kazi**	**female** teacher
	uMnumzana	Mr
	uNkosikazi	Mrs
–	**in**kosikazi	lady

Verbs

-thenga	buy
-tsha	burn
-khangela	look at/for, check
-galela	pour in/out/on
-ncedisa	help, assist
-dlala	play
-sela	drink (cold)
-phunga	drink (hot)
-tya	eat
-vuthuza	blow
-tshintsha	change
-buza	ask (a question)
-hlamba	wash

General

eMzantsi Afrika	**in** South Africa
kukho	there is/are ...
phaya	over there
kamnandi	nicely, pleasantly
kakhulu	a lot, very
(nga)phandle	outside
(nga)phakathi	inside
kodwa	but
kumama	**from** mother
ahleli/**ba**hleli	**they** are sitting/**they** are living
gqitha	a lot, excessively, too much
-khe	his/her

Instructions •
Noun Classes 9 & 10 (with Verb Links)

1. Instructions

Positive instructions

Singular (when speaking to one person)
The **stem** of the verb is used:

Hamba!	Go!
Sebenza!	Work!
Ngena!	Come in!
Hlala phantsi!	Sit down!
Thetha isiXhosa!	Speak Xhosa!

Plural (when speaking to more than one person)
The **stem + ni** is used.

Hambani!
Sebenzani!
Ngenani!
Hlalani phantsi!
Thethani isiXhosa!

Ngenani!

NOTE

The _tone_ of the voice shows whether the instruction is gentle or severe.

Umsebenzi 1

Write the following instructions in the plural and then translate

1. Nceda
2. Hamba
3. Sebenza
4. Goduka
5. Jonga

6. Thula
7. Vuka
8. Phakama
9. Mamela
10. Phulaphula

NOTE

- **-nceda**   help
  -ncedisa   help/assist someone
- **-mamela**   listen (to)
  -phulaphula listen (to), pay attention

Public address systems such as those at railway stations use 'Phulaphulani!' to attract attention of commuters.

Umsebenzi 2

Translate into Xhosa (singular and plural)

1. Come in
2. Sit down
3. Go well
4. Stay well
5. Pour (in) water
6. Buy bread
7. Wash the car
8. Help the woman
9. Call the children
10. Look here

NB When addressing someone **directly**, as in a greeting or instruction, the initial vowel of that noun is dropped.

Ngena, Sipho!   Come in Sipho
Ngenani, bantwana   Come in children

Umsebenzi 3

Translate into Xhosa

1. Look Nomsa
2. Wake up children
3. Go well Themba
4. Stay well Lizo and friends
5. Listen (attention) students
6. Get up young man
7. Be quiet children
8. Listen well child
9. Sit down 'lady'/ma'am
10. Sit down gentlemen

Exceptions

- If the verb stem has only one syllable, **yi-** is placed before it.
  Yitya!   Eat
  Yiza!   Come
- If the verb stem begins with a vowel, **y-** is placed before it.
  Yenza iti!   Make tea
- **Plural**: Add **-ni**
  Yitya**ni**!   Eat
  Yiza**ni**!   Come
  Yenza**ni** iti!   Make tea

Umsebenzi 4

Fill in the correct form of the verb in brackets

1. Mntwana, ... (eat)
2. Bantwana, ... (eat)
3. Themba, ... (come) here
4. Bafana, ... (come) here
5. Nomsa, ... (make) tea

NOTE

Yiza apha	→	Yiz' apha!	Come here
Yenza iti	→	Yenz' iti!	Make tea

Umsebenzi 5

Fill in a suitable verb from the list below and then translate (singular)

-vula, -enza, -ya, -funda, -hlala, -sela, -za, -mamela, -vala, -tya

1. .... phantsi!
2. .... apha!
3. .... iCoke!
4. .... ifestile!
5. .... incwadi!
6. .... iti!
7. .... ucango!
8. .... isidudu!
9. .... abazali!
10. .... e**venkileni**! (**to** the shop)

NOTE

There is no word for **please** in Xhosa. However the verb **-nceda** (help) may be used to express please. The verb which follows, takes the verb link and ends in **-e**.

Singular	Nceda, **u**phind**e**!	Please repeat
Plural	Ncedani, **ni**phind**e**!	Please repeat

Negative instructions

Listen to the following on the tape and repeat

Singular

Musa ukuhamba!	Do not go
Musa ukungena!	Do not enter
Musa ukusebenza!	Do not work
Musa ukugoduka	Do not go home
Musa ukuza namhlanje!	Do not come today

Plural

Musani ukuhamba!	Do not go
Musani ukungena!	Do not enter
Musani ukusebenza!	Do not work
Musani ukugoduka!	Do not go home
Musani ukuza namhlanje!	Do not come today

N O T E

- **Musa + uku-** is a construction and thus **uku-** is not translated as **to**.

- The verb stems which are exceptions in **positive** instructions, are treated normally in the **negative**.

Umsebenzi 6

Put the following instructions into the negative (singular and plural) and translate

1. Thetha!
2. Jonga!
3. Dlala ngaphandle!
4. Yiya ngoku!
5. Yiza ngomso!

Umsebenzi 7

Translate the following instructions into Xhosa

1. Speak Xhosa — Do not speak English
2. Close the window — Do not close the door
3. Ask father — Do not ask mother
4. Call the doctor — Do not call Lizo
5. Come today — Do not come tomorrow

Put the above instructions into the plural

Umsebenzi 8

Translate the following negative instructions (singular)
1. Do not forget
2. Do not lie
3. Do not make a noise
4. Do not laugh
5. Do not cry

NOTE

In everyday spoken Xhosa the negative form is generally shortened:

Singular	**Suku**hamba!	**Don't** go
Plural	**Sanuku**hamba!	**Don't** go
NB	**Sukukhawulezisa!**	Don't hurry (with your speech); speak slowly
	Zekelela!	Can also be used for 'speak slowly'

Summary of Instructions

	Singular	Plural
Positive	Hamba! **Y**iza! **Y**enza iti!	Hamba**ni**! Yiza**ni**! Yenza**ni** iti!
Negative	**Musa uku**hamba! **Musa uku**za! **Musa ukw**enza iti!	**Musani uku**hamba! **Musani uku**za! **Musani ukw**enza iti!
Short form	**Suku**hamba!	**Sanuku**hamba!

INCOKO

Ukusebenza ekhaya   *Working at home*
Abantwana bancedisa abazali ekhaya

Umama:	**Yizani** bantwana! Kukho umsebenzi kakhulu namhlanje!
Abantwana:	Kulungile mama! Siyeza!
Umama:	Utata ufuna ukuhlamba imoto. Themba, **musa ukudlala** ngoku. **Ncedisa** utata. **Yiya** phandle.
UThemba:	Kulungile mama! Ndiyaya.

Umama:	Nomsa, **musa ukulibala** ukukhupha inkunkuma! Emva koko, **tshayela** umgangatho apha ekhitshini. Mna, ndihlamba iimpahla phakathi.
UNomsa:	Kulungile mama!
	Bonke bayasebenza

NOTE

Siy<u>e</u>za   We are coming.

a   →   **e** before the verb **-za** (come)

Bonke bayasebenza

Umsebenzi 9

a) *Phendula imibuzo*
1. Abantwana bancedisa bani?
2. Utata ufuna uk**w**enza ntoni?
3. UThemba uncedisa bani?
4. Utata noThemba basebenza phi?
5. UNomsa ukhupha ntoni?
6. UNomsa **w**enza ntoni ekhitshini?
7. Umama **w**enza ntoni?
8. Bonke **b**enza ntoni?
9. Kulungile ukuncedisa abazali?
10. Wena, uyanceda ekhaya? **W**enza ntoni?

b) Translate this passage into Xhosa

Mother calls the children. There is a lot of work today. They come. Themba helps father outside. They wash the car. Nomsa takes out the rubbish. After that she sweeps the floor in the kitchen. Mother washes the clothes inside. They are all working.

NOTE

- Some verb stems begin with a vowel:

  -enza   make, do
  ukwenza   **to** make, do

- Xhosa does not allow two vowels to stand together. Thus when another vowel comes before **-enza:**

ndi-	→	**nd-**	**Nd**enza ntoni?	What am **I** doing?
u-	→	**w-**	**W**enza ntoni?	What are **you** doing?
si-	→	**s-**	**S**enza ntoni?	What are **we** doing?
ni-	→	**n-**	**N**enza ntoni?	What are **you** doing?
Umama u-	→	**w-**	Umama **w**enza ntoni?	
Abantu ba-	→	**b-**	Abantu **b**enza ntoni?	

Thus

- Where there is a consonant + vowel in the link, drop the vowel.
- Where there is a vowel only in the link, **u-** → **w**.

- Verb stems can begin with the vowels a, e, or o:

ukwakha	**to** build	u → w before **a**
ukwenza	**to** make, do	u → w before **e**
ukoyika	**to** be afraid	**u** falls away before **o**

- Negative instructions

Musa ukwakha indlu!	Do not build a house
Musa ukwenza iti!	Do not make tea
Musa ukoyika!	Do not be afraid

2. Noun Classes 9 & 10

There are many nouns in Classes 9 & 10.
There are *three* possible prefixes for Class 9 nouns and *four* for Class 10 nouns.
The prefix used depends on the *stem* of the noun.

Most borrowed words (from English and Afrikaans)

Prefixes: i- &   ii-

Class 9 (singular)	**Class 10** (plural)	
imoto	**ii**moto	car
ifestile	**ii**festile	window
ifani	**ii**fani	surname
ivenkile	**ii**venkile	shop
igaraji	**ii**garaji	garage

imoto

Noun stems of Xhosa origin

Prefixes: in- &   iin-/izin-

* **Stems of two or more syllables**

incwadi	**iin**cwadi	book
intombi	**iin**tombi	girl
indaba	**iin**daba	matter (singular)
		news (plural)

* **Stems of one syllable**

indlu	**izin**dlu	house
inja	**izin**ja	dog
into	**izin**to	thing

NB The **z** of **izin-** is very significant. It always indicates plural.   *inja*

Noun stems of Xhosa origin which begin with b, p, f or v

Prefixes: im- &   iim-

imbongi	**iim**bongi	oral poet
impahla	**iim**pahla	goods, clothes, belongings
imfene	**iim**fene	baboon
imvula	**iim**vula	rain

NB

* **b, p, f** and **v** are all sounds made by using the lips.
* **n** → **m** before these sounds.

NOTE

Both **Class 5** and **Class 9** nouns can prefix **i-**.

If the stem is of Xhosa origin, it is usually in Class 5.

ixesha	amaxesha	5 & 6	time

If the stem is a borrowed word, it is usually in Class 9.

imoto	iimoto	9 & 10	car

However, there are exceptions, for example: *(See p. 22)*

itikiti	amatikiti	5 & 6	ticket

NB Classes 9 & 6

A few nouns in Class 9 prefix **ama-** in the plural.

indoda	amadoda	man
*inkosikazi	amakhosikazi	lady/wife
*inkosazana	amakhosazana	miss
*inkwenkwe	amakhwenkwe	boy
intombazana	amantombazana	little girl

*An **h** is always dropped if there is an **n** in the previous syllable of a word.

Umsebenzi 10

Give the plural form of the following nouns with their classes, and translate

1. ivenkile
2. igama
3. incwadi
4. ibhasi
5. ipolisa
6. ikati
7. inja
8. impuku
9. idolophu
10. ithuba

NOTE

Ido*l*ophu (town) comes from the Afrikaans **dorp**.

In the past, the **r** of borrowed words was often pronounced as **l**. However, this is changing, with the **r** being retained in many words.

ibrukhwe	*for*	ibhulukwe	trousers
isitrato		isitalato	street
-duru		-dulu	expensive
iMerika		iMelika	America

Fill in the appropriate noun and translate

1.	Ndifunda	(a book)
2.	Lumkela .... apha	(danger)
3.	Vala	(the windows)
4.	Ufuna .... **yo**kutya?	(a thing/something)
5.	Ufuna .... okanye ....?	(tea) (coffee)
6.	Abantu bafuna	(houses)
7.	Mamelani	(the news)
8.	Sithenga .... egaraji	(petrol)
9.	Khupha	(the rubbish)
10.	Musa ukulibala .... zakho	(belongings)

Verb Links: Classes 9 & 10

Study the following examples (Class 9 nouns)

1.	**I**kati **i**sela ubisi	The cat (it) drinks milk
2.	**In**doda **i**sebenza eKapa	The man (he) works in Cape Town
3.	**In**tombi **i**yafunda	The girl (she) is studying
4.	**In**ja **i**yabaleka	The dog (it) is running
5.	**Im**vula **i**yeza!	The rain (it) is coming

N O T E

Once again it is clear that the verb link is derived from the prefix of the noun.
The **Verb Link** for all **Class 9** nouns is **i-** (he, she or it).

Study the following examples (Class 10 nouns)

1.	**Ii**kati **zi**sela ubisi	Cats (they) drink milk
2.	**Ii**bhasi **zi**ya eMonti	The buses (they) are going to East London
3.	**Iin**tombi **zi**yafunda	The girls (they) are studying
4.	**Izin**ja **zi**yabaleka	The dogs (they) are running
5.	**Iim**puku **zi**ngena ekhitshini	The mice (they) enter the kitchen

N O T E

The verb link is derived from the *basic* prefix of Class 10, **izin-**.
The **Verb Link** for all **Class 10** nouns is **zi-** (they).

Umsebenzi 12

Fill in the correct verb link and translate

1. Ibhasi ......yafika
2. Iimoto ......yahamba
3. Iintombi ......phendula ititshalakazi
4. Inkosikazi ......ncedisa umakhulu
5. Izinja ......bona ikati
6. Indoda ......funda incwadi
7. Amantombazana ......yaphakama
8. Ititshala ......buza imibuzo
9. Inkwenkwe ......yadlala
10. Amakhwenkwe ......yadlala

NOTE

utitshala(kazi)   1a   a certain teacher (personal)
ititshala(kazi)   9   a teacher (impersonal)
-kazi is a feminine ending, as in inkosi**kazi**.

Umsebenzi 13

Fill in the correct verb link and the word in brackets. Translate.

1. Indoda ...hlamba .... (the car)
2. Iintombi ...thenga .... (sweets)
3. Inkwenkwe ...vela .... (from school)
4. Iinkomo ...sela .... (water)
5. Intombazana ...tshayela .... (the floor)
6. Iibhasi ...hamba .... (tomorrow)
7. Imoto ...vela .... (from Johannesburg)
8. Izinja ...luma .... (people)
9. Iikati ...thanda .... (mice)
10. Inkosikazi ...cela .... (money)

NOTE

- **-buza**   ask (a question)
  -cela   ask (for something)

- With the verb **-e**nza (make, do) the verb link changes as follows:
  i-   →   y-
  zi-   →   z-
  Intombi **y**enza ntoni?   What is the girl doing?
  Iintombi **z**enza ntoni?   What are the girls doing?

INCOKO

Inkwenkwe ilesa incwadi   *A boy is reading a book.*

Umakhulu:	Molo mzukulwana! **W**enza ntoni?
Inkwenkwe:	Molo makhulu! Ndifunda incwadi.
Umakhulu:	Oo, ndiyabona. Kukho imifanekiso?
Inkwenkwe:	Ewe, makhulu. Jonga!
	Umakhulu ujonga imifanekiso.
Umakhulu:	Awu! Indoda **y**enza ntoni apha?
Inkwenkwe:	Iyapeynta. Ipeynta indlu.
Umakhulu:	Inkwenkwe **y**enza ntoni?
Inkwenkwe:	Ibamba ileri. Incedisa utata.
Umakhulu:	Iintombi **z**enza ntoni?
Inkwenkwe:	Ziyadlala.
Umakhulu:	Inkosikazi **y**enza ntoni?
Inkwenkwe:	Iyapheka. Ipheka ekhitshini.
Umakhulu:	Awu! Bonke **b**onwabile!
Inkwenkwe:	Ewe makhulu, **b**onwabile!

Umsebenzi 14

Phendula imibuzo

1. Inkwenkwe ibulisa bani?
2. Inkwenkwe **y**enza ntoni?
3. Kukho imifanekiso encwadini?
4. Indoda **y**enza ntoni emfanekisweni?
5. Inkwenkwe **y**enza ntoni?
6. Iintombi **z**enza ntoni?
7. Inkosikazi **y**enza ntoni?
8. Ipheka phi?
9. Bonke **b**onwabile?
10. Wena, **w**onwabile namhlanje?

NOTE

-onwabile	**be happy**
Ndonwabile	**I** am happy
Wonwabile	**You** are happy (also: he, she)
Bonwabile	**They** are happy

Translate this passage into Xhosa

The boy is reading a book. There are pictures in the book. Grandmother greets the boy. They look at the pictures. They see a man. He is painting the house. A boy is helping. He is holding the ladder. The girls are playing. The lady is cooking. She is cooking in the kitchen. They are all happy.

NOTE

As mentioned earlier, **age** plays a very important part in the lives of the Xhosa people. This fact is borne out in the vocabulary, which contains a rich variety of words for all the stages of development.

inkwenkwe (boy)   **intombazana** (little girl)
umfana (young man)   **intombi** (girl, young woman)
indoda (man)   **umfazi** (a married woman)

INCOKO
Egaraji   *At the Garage*

Umsebenzi:	Molo nkosikazi!
Inkosikazi:	Molo mnumzana!
Umsebenzi:	Kunjani namhlanje?
Inkosikazi:	Kulungile/Sikhona, enkosi. Kunjani kuwe?
Umsebenzi:	Hayi, ndisaphila, enkosi. Ndi**nga**ku**nceda**?
Inkosikazi:	Ewe, enkosi. Nceda, **uzalise itanki.**
Umsebenzi:	Kulungile. Ndicela isitshixo.
Inkosikazi:	Oo, uxolo. Nasi!
	Umsebenzi uzalisa itanki.
Umsebenzi:	Injani ioyile nkosikazi?
Inkosikazi:	Nceda, **ukhangele ioyile, ibhetri namanzi.**
Umsebenzi:	Kulungile. **Khawu**vul**e** ibhonethi.
	Inkosikazi ivula ibhonethi. Umsebenzi ukhangela yonke into.

Umsebenzi:	Yonke into ilungile nkosikazi.
Inkosikazi:	Enkosi.
Umsebenzi:	Anjani amavili?
Inkosikazi:	Nceda, **umpompe amavili** nge 2 bar.
	Umsebenzi umpompa amavili.
Umsebenzi:	Zinjani iifestile?
Inkosikazi:	Awu, zimdaka kakhulu! Nceda, **usule iifestile**!
	Umsebenzi usula iifestile.
Umsebenzi:	Ndigqibile nkosikazi!
Inkosikazi:	Enkosi kakhulu mnumzana. **Yimalini**?
Umsebenzi:	Yi R200 kanye.
Inkosikazi:	Yho! Ipetroli idulu! Nantsi imali! **Le yeyakho**!
Umsebenzi:	Enkosi kakhulu nkosikazi. Hamba kakuhle!
Inkosikazi:	Sala kakuhle mnumzana!

NOTE

- Try to adapt this conversation to suit your own needs. For example, use the greetings of your choice. Note the following variations:

Galela ipetroli ngeR50!	**for**	Zalisa itanki!
Amafutha		Ioyile
Unjani umoya?		Anjani amavili?
Nali ikhadi!		Nantsi imali!

- Notice the use of the verb link with parts of speech other than the verb. The link then introduces the appropriate verb.

Injani ioyile?	How **is** the oil?
Zinjani iifestile?	How **are** the windows?
Ipetroli **i**dulu	Petrol **is** expensive
Iifestile **zi**mdaka	The windows **are** dirty

- An alternative way of saying **please** is
  khawu- + verb ending in **-e**.

Khawuzalis**e** itanki!	**Please** fill the tank
Khawusul**e** iifestile!	**Please** wipe the windows

> .....Zalisa itanki
> ....Khangela ioyile, ibhetri namanzi
> ... Mpompa amavili
> ... Sula iifestile

THE ROLE OF THE XHOSA ORAL POET

The **imbongi** or oral poet has been described as someone who lived in close proximity to a chief and who accompanied the chief on important occasions. His performance would be directed at the chief, decrying what was unworthy, praising what was worthy and even forecasting what was going to happen. Clearly the **imbongi's** role was one which allowed for criticism.

A poet praiser has to be found credible by the community. They appoint him, and he becomes the voice of the community, representing the grassroots feeling of the people. Today, **iimbongi** produce praises at various functions such as graduation ceremonies, retirement parties, the opening of schools, crèches, clinics and so on. But the most highly-regarded praises are those produced in honour of political organisations and political leaders, including those who align themselves with the organisations. The reason for this would seem to be that it is now these organisations and to a large extent no longer the 'traditional' chiefs, which are important in the lives of the people.

Power and the Poet (in Contemporary Transkei)
by Russell Kaschula

ISIGAMA

Nouns

Class		
9 & 10	iti	tea
	ikofu	coffee
	imoto	car
	ifestile	window
	ivenkile	shop
	igaraji	garage
	ibhasi	bus
	ikati	cat
	idolophu	town
	ipetroli	petrol
	ititshala(kazi)	teacher (f.)
	ilekese	sweet
	imali	money
	ileri	ladder
	indlu	house
	inja	dog

	into	thing
	incoko	conversation
	ingoma	song
	inkosi	chief, lord, master
	incwadi	book, letter
	inkunkuma	rubbish
	intombi	girl, daughter
	indaba	matter (sg), news (pl)
	inkomo	cow, bull, ox; cattle (pl)
	ingozi	danger, accident
	imbongi	oral poet, poet praiser
	impahla	clothes, belongings (sg or pl)
	imfene	baboon
	imvula	rain
	impuku	mouse
9 & 6	**in**doda	man
	inkosikazi	lady, wife
	inkosazana	miss
	inkwenkwe	boy
	intombazana	young girl
3 & 4	**um**gangatho	floor
	umfanekiso	picture
1 & 2	**um**zukulwana	grandchild
5 & 6	**i**thuba	chance, opportunity
–	**u**cango	door
–	**u**bisi	milk
9 & 10	**i**tanki	tank
	ioyile	oil
	ibhetri	battery
	ibhonethi	bonnet
7 & 8	**isi**tya	dish
	isitshixo	key
5 & 6	**i**khadi	card

Verbs

-ngena	go/come in
-nceda	help
-jonga	look/look at
-thula	be quiet
-vuka	wake up
-phakama	get/stand up
-mamela	listen
-phulaphula	pay attention
-biza	call
-phinda	repeat
-za	come
-vula	open
-vala	close
-libala	forget
-xoka	lie
-ngxola	make a noise
-hleka	laugh/laugh at
-lila	cry (shed tears)
-khawuleza	hurry
-khawulezisa	hurry up, do quickly
-zekelela	be slow, tardy
-khupha	take out
-tshayela	sweep
-phendula	answer
-akha	build
-enza	make, do
-oyika	be afraid of, fear
-onwaba	be/become happy
-lumkela	beware of
-baleka	run
-fika	arrive
-luma	bite
-cela	ask for something, request
-peynta/peyinta	paint
-bamba	hold
-pheka	cook
-bulisa	greet
-zalisa	fill
-mpompa	pump
-sula	wipe

General

phantsi	down, below
apha	here
nceda	please
e**venkileni**	**to/at** the shop
ngomso	tomorrow
siy**eza**	we are coming
emva koko	after that
e**khitshini**	**in** the kitchen
bonke	all (with Class 2/2a nouns)
noThemba	**and** Themba
into **yo**kutya	something 'to' eat
into **yo**kusela	something 'to' drink (cold)
into **yo**kuphunga	something 'to' drink (hot)
zakho	your (with Class 8/10 nouns)
okanye	or
e**sikolweni**	**from** school
awu!	gee!
-onwabile	be happy
e**ncwadini**	**in** the book
e**mfanekisweni**	**in** the picture
Nd**inga**kunceda?	**Can** I help <u>you</u>?
uxolo	sorry
na**si**	here **it** is (Class 7 nouns)
namanzi	**and** water
yonke into	**every** thing
-lungile	good, fine
nge 2 bar	**with** 2 bars
-mdaka	dirty
ndigqib**ile**	I **have** finished
Yimal**ini**?	**What** money is it? (How much is it?)
kanye	exactly
-dulu	expensive
nantsi	here **it** is (Class 9 nouns)
le yeyakho	**this** is yours
na**li**	here **it** is (Class 5 nouns)
khawu ... e	**please** + verb

Summary

The three main constructions dealt with thus far are
Statements
Questions
Instructions

Statements

Ndi**ya**funda	I am studying
Ndifunda **isiXhosa**	I am studying **Xhosa**

Questions

- **No 'question word'**   (Answer **yes** or **no**)
  U**ya**funda?   Are you studying?
  Ufunda **isiXhosa?**   Are you studying **Xhosa?**

- **With a 'question word'**   (Cannot answer yes or no!)
  Ufunda **ntoni?**   **What** are you studying?
  Ufuna **bani?**   **Whom** do you want?
  Uphila **njani?**   **How** are you?
  Uvela **phi?**   **Where** do you come from?
  Uhamba **nini?**   **When** are you going?

Instructions

- **Positive**

Singular	**Plural**	
Hamba!	Hamba**ni!**	Go
Yiza!	**Yi**za**ni!**	Come
Yenza iti!	**Y**enza**ni** iti!	Make tea

- **Negative**

Musa ukuhamba!	**Musani uku**hamba!	Do not go
Musa ukuza!	**Musani uku**za!	Do not come
Musa ukwenza iti!	**Musani ukw**enza iti!	Do not make tea

- **Colloquial**

Sukuhamba!	**Sanuku**hamba!	Don't go

- When addressing someone **directly,** the first vowel of that noun is always dropped.

Molo mnumzana!	Hullo 'mister'/sir
Molweni banumzana!	Hullo gentlemen
Yiz' apha Themba!	Come here Themba
Yizani apha Themba!	Come here Themba and others
Ewe, mama!	Yes, mother
Enkosi, tata!	Thank you, father

- **Two vowels may not stand together** in Xhosa. There are two exceptions:
  - Class 2a prefix   **oo**Themba
  - Class 10 prefix   **ii**ncwadi

This rule does not apply to borrowed words.

ioyile (oil), iapile (apple), iofisi (office)

In all other cases, when two vowels do come together, a change must be made. For example, with the verb **-enza** (make, do), the verb link:

- loses its vowel   **N**enza ntoni?   (ni → n)

                                                          Benza ntoni?   (ba → b)
- a single vowel becomes a consonant   **W**enza ntoni?   (u → w)

                                                          Yenza ntoni?   (i → y)

Summary of Noun Classes 1 to 10

Person	Noun	Noun Prefix	Verb Link	
1st			ndi-	si-
2nd			u-	ni-
3rd (Classes)				
1	**um**ntu	um-	u-	
2	**aba**ntu	aba-	ba-	
1a	**u**tata	u-	u-	
2a	**oo**tata	oo-	ba-	
3	**um**sebenzi	um-	u-	
4	**imi**sebenzi	imi-	i-	
5	**ili**fu	ili-	li-	
	igama	i- }		
6	**ama**fu: **ama**gama	ama-	a-	
7	**isi**tshixo	isi-	si-	
8	**izi**tshixo	izi-	zi-	
9	**i**festile	i-		
	incwadi: **in**ja	in- }	i-	
	impahla	im-		
10	**ii**festile	ii-		
	iincwadi	iin- }	zi-	
	izinja	izin-		
	iimpahla	iim-		

NOTE

The **Verb Link** is derived from the *noun prefix* as follows:
- It always takes the **vowel** of the prefix
- If there is a **consonant** in the basic prefix, it is placed before the vowel (**m** and **n** are considered **nasals** and not consonants, they are therefore ignored in this case).
- Classes 1a & 2a are subsidiary classes of 1 & 2 and therefore take the same links.

Points of Interest

1. The Body (Umzimba)

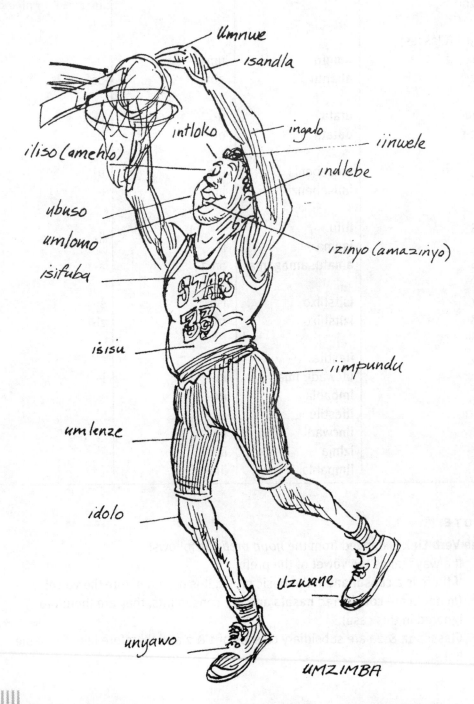

Umnwe
isandla
intloko
ingalo
iinwele
iliso (amehlo)
indlebe
ubuso
umlomo
izinyo (amazinyo)
isifuba
isisu
iimpundu
umlenze
idolo
uzwane
unyawo

UMZIMBA

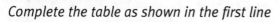

Complete the table as shown in the first line

Classes	Singular	Plural	Meaning
3 & 4	**um**zimba	**imi**zimba	body
	intloko		
14	**ubu**so	–	
11 & 10	(unwele)		
	iliso		
	impumlo		
	umlomo		
	izinyo		
	indlebe		
	intamo		
	igxalaba		
	isifuba		
	ingalo		
	isandla		
	umnwe		
	isisu		
	(**im**pundu)		
	umlenze		
	idolo		
11 & 10	**u**nyawo		
11 & 10	**u**zwane		

UMHOBE • POEM

Vul' impompo!	Open the pump!
Val' impompo!	Close the pump!
Yiz' apha!	Come here!
Yiz' apha!	Come here!
Ndithath' isepha	I take soap
Ndihlamb' izandla	I wash hands
Ubuso, iindlebe.	Face, ears.

2. Occupations (Imisebenzi)

1	**um**bhali	writer
1	**um**bhali-mali	accountant
1a	**u**nobhala	secretary
1a	**u**mantyi	magistrate
5	**i**gqwetha	lawyer
1	**um**cuphi	detective
5	**i**joni	soldier
1	**um**sasazi	announcer
1	**um**ongameli	president
9	**in**kulumbuso	prime minister
9	**in**qununu	principal
1	**um**qeqeshi	trainer, coach

Umsebenzi 2

What are the following occupations? Translate and give the class

1. **u**noncwadi
2. **u**novenkile
3. **u**noposi
4. **u**noderi
5. **u**noteksi

6. **u**makheniki
7. **i**njineli
8. **i**jaji
9. **um**ongikazi
10. **u**gqirha wamazinyo

"Okay, how do you say 'Hou links' in Venda?"

3. Public Signs

Umsebenzi 3

Match the following signs with their English equivalents

1. Ingozi	Private property
2. Musa ukulahla inkunkuma apha	Exit
3. Akungenwa	No smoking
4. Akutshaywa	Beware of the dog!
5. Uxolo! Imisebenzi! Inkululeko!	Danger
6. Ngumhlaba womntu lo	No dumping here
7. Kungenwa apha	Information
8. Lumkela inja	No entry
9. Kuphunywa apha	Entrance
10. Ukwazisa/Ukwaziswa	Peace! Jobs! Freedom!

4. Interesting Words

radio	9	**i**radiyo	from 'radio'
	9	**i**wayilesi	from 'wireless'
	1a	**u**nomathotholo	association of voices coming from a box
television	9	**i**televizhini	from 'television'
	1a	**u**mabonakude	-bona (see) + kude (far away)
movie	9	**i**bhayoskophu	from 'bioscope'
	9	**i**filimu	from 'film'
pension	3	**um**hlalaphantsi	-hlala (sit) + phantsi (down)
motorbike	7	**isi**thuthuthu	from the sound a motorbike makes!
aeroplane	9	**in**qwelomoya	wagon of the wind
	9	**i**eropleni	from 'aeroplane'

Idonkirabhijezi   Zebra (literally, a donkey with a striped rugby jersey!)

This word comes from **Fanakalo,** a compound language developed on the mines to facilitate communication. It means 'similar to that one' because various languages were compounded, with the aim of making them similar to one another.

idonkirabhijezi

ISIGAMA

Nouns

Classes

3 & 4	**um**zimba	body
	umlomo	mouth
	umnwe	finger
	umlenze	leg
5 & 6	**ili**so & **ame**hlo	eye
	igxalaba & **ama**gxa	shoulder
	izinyo	tooth
	idolo	knee
7 & 8	**isi**fuba	chest
	isisu	stomach
	isandla	hand
9 & 10	**in**tloko	head
	indlebe	ear
	intamo	neck
	ingalo	arm
	impumlo	nose
	(**im-**) **iim**pundu	buttocks
11 & 10	(**u-**) **iin**wele	hair
	unyawo & **iin**yawo	foot
	uzwane & **iin**zwane	toe
14	**ubu**so	face
3 & 4	**um**hobe	poem
9 & 10	**im**pompo	pump
	isepha	soap
	ingozi	danger, accident
	inkululeko	freedom
11	**u**xolo	peace
3 & 4	**um**hlaba	land, soil, earth

Verbs

-thatha	take
-lahla	throw away
-tshaya	smoke
-lumkela	beware of
-phuma	go out, come out
-azisa	make known, inform

NOTE

Vocabulary for Occupations and Interesting Words: See pages 58 and 60.

Place • Time • Counting

1. Expressing Place (from nouns)

Study the following familiar examples

Ndihlala **e**khaya	I live **at** home
Ndivela **ku**mama	I (have) come **from** mother
Ndiya **e**msebenz**ini**	I am going **to** work

In English we use prepositions
(in, on, at, to, from, etc.) to express **place**.
There are no prepositions in Xhosa.
Instead, the form of the noun changes in
various ways, as seen above.

NOTE

The meaning of the English preposition
depends on:

• The **verb** in the sentence

Sivela **e**Goli	We come **from** Johannesburg
Siya **e**Goli	We are going **to** Johannesburg
Sihlala **e**Goli	We live **in** Johannesburg

• The **context** in which the verb is used

Sihlala **e**khaya	We live **at** home
Sihlala **e**fama	We live **on** a farm
Sihlala **e**Kapa	We live **in** Cape Town

The three main constructions used to express Place from Nouns

1. Some Nouns replace their initial vowel with E-

- **Most place names**

i**K**apa	→	e**K**apa	**in** Cape Town
i**G**oli	→	e**G**oli	**to** Johannesburg
i**B**hayi	→	e**B**hayi	**from** Port Elizabeth
i**M**onti	→	e**M**onti	**at** East London
i**K**himbali	→	e**K**himbali	**from** Kimberley
i**P**itoli	→	e**P**itoli	**to** Pretoria

Also: **e**Rondebosch, **e**New Brighton, **e**Mdantsane, **e**Soweto, **e**Gugulethu, **e**Nyanga

NOTE

- **e**Rhawut**ini** (from Afrikaans 'goud') is another name for **e**Goli.
- **e**Gaut**eng** – **in** the Gauteng Province (This is the Sotho spelling).
- **Soweto** is an acronym for **So**uth **We**stern **T**ownships.
- u**M**zantsi Afrika → e**M**zantsi Afrika   **in** South Africa
  i**M**elika → e**M**elika   **from** America
  i**N**gilani → e**N**gilani   **to** England

- **Certain Special Nouns**

i**kh**aya	→	e**kh**aya	**at** home
i**g**araji	→	e**g**araji	**to** the garage
i**s**ibhedlele	→	e**s**ibhedlele	**in** hospital
i**kh**emesti	→	e**kh**emesti	**from** the chemist
i**f**ama	→	e**f**ama	**on** a farm
i**y**univesithi	→	e**y**univesithi	**at** university
i**n**tloko	→	e**n**tloko	**on** the head
u**l**wandle	→	e**l**wandle	**in** the sea

NOTE

- This applies only to certain nouns. There is no particular reason they prefix an **e-** only.
- The **e-** denotes **time** in the following two words:

i**m**ini	→	e**m**ini	**in** the day
u**b**usuku	→	e**b**usuku	**at** night

Umsebenzi 1

Fill in the correct form of the noun in brackets and translate
1. Umama usebenza (ikhaya)
2. Utata uthenga ipetroli (igaraji)
3. Kumnandi ukuhlala (ifama)
4. OoMazibuko bavela (iBhayi) kodwa bahlala (iKápa) ngoku
5. (Imini) siyasebenza kodwa (ubusuku) siyalala

Umsebenzi 2

Phendula: Wena ...
1. Uvela phi?
2. Uhlala phi?
3. Uya phi ngoku?   (to the garage)
4. Uvela phi ngoku?   (from the chemist)
5. Ufunda phi?   (at university)

NOTE

Kwa- is prefixed to nouns of Classes 1a and 2a to express at, in, to, from, **the house, place or property of ...**

kwaThemba	**at** Themba's house
kwatata	**at** father's house
kwaMazibuko	**at** the Mazibukos' house
kwaZulu	**in** the land of Zulu
kwaLanga	**in** Langa

- Zulu and Langa were both chiefs, hence these place names take **kwa-** and not e-.

- Companies, businesses, shops, etc. can also prefix **kwa-**, indicating the property of ...
  kwaShell
  kwaWoolworths

- **kwa**gqirha   **at the place of** the doctor
  compare
  kugqirha   **to/from** the doctor (wherever he/she may be)

2. Class 1a and 2a Nouns prefix K-

Class 1a

kuThemba	**to** Themba
kumama	**from** mother
kuThixo	**to** God
kunomathotholo	**on** the radio

Class 2a

kooThemba	**to** Themba and friends
kootata	**from** father and company
koosisi	**from** sister and others
kooSiyengo	**to** the Siyengo family

Umsebenzi 3

Fill in the correct form of the noun in brackets and translate

1. Sivela (umakhulu) ngoku
2. Siya (ooMadala) ngomso
3. Umntwana uya (ugqirha) namhlanje
4. Sicela uncedo (uThixo)
5. Utata uthanda ukumamela iindaba (unomathotholo)

NOTE

Ndiya **ku**Themba	I am going to Themba (he may be anywhere)
Ndiya **kwa**Themba	I am going to Themba's home (he is the owner)

3. All Other Nouns

- Replace the initial vowel with **e-**.
- Replace the final vowel as follows:

-a	→	-**eni**	intaba	→	entab**eni**	**to** the mountain
-e	→	-**eni**	itafile	→	etafil**eni**	**on** the table
-i	→	-**ini**	igadi	→	egad**ini**	**in** the garden
-o	→	-**weni**	isikolo	→	esikol**weni**	**at** school
-u	→	-**wini**	indlu	→	endl**wini**	**from** the house

Learn **-eni, -eni, -ini, -weni, -wini** as a rhyme, to correspond with the five vowels. Then learn each of the above examples to perfection in order to facilitate getting a feel for the endings of nouns in general. It will come naturally after a while.

Change these nouns so that they express place. Give an English translation

1.	isonka	6.	iphepha
2.	ivenkile	7.	iposi
3.	ibhanki	8.	iketile
4.	imoto	9.	isitulo
5.	umsebenzi	10.	igumbi

NOTE

- **Exceptions**

  ikofu   :   Ufuna ubisi eko**fini**?

  idolophu   :   Ndiya edoloph**ini**

- amaXhosa   **e**maXhoseni   **in/from** the 'land of the Xhosas'

  compare   :   **kwa**Zulu   **in/from** the 'land of Zulu'

Give the correct form of the noun in brackets and translate

1. Bhala igama lakho (incwadi)!
2. UMary ubeka ukutya (itafile)
3. Utata usebenza (idolophu)
4. Ndibona umhlobo (indlela)
5. Sukuhamba (imvula)!
6. Kushushu kakhulu (ilanga) namhlanje
7. Ikati ithanda ukulala (ibhedi)
8. Kukho abantu abaninzi (intolongo)
9. Jonga iintaka (umthi)!
10. Abantu bakhwela (ibhasi)

UThemba ukhwela ebhasini

NOTE

- UThemba ukhwela **ibhasi**   Themba catches **the bus**

  UThemba ukhwela **ebhasini**   Themba gets **on/into the bus**

- In order to differentiate between a Class 9 and a Class 10 noun, when expressing place, the letter **z** is used with Class 10 nouns.

  incwadi   →   encwadini   in the book

  iincwadi   →   e**z**incwadini   in the books

Umsebenzi 6

Complete the following, using nouns which express place
1. Umntu uthenga ipetroli ....
2. Umntu utsala imali...
3. Umntu uthenga izitampu ....
4. Umntu uthenga iyeza ....
5. Umntu uthenga iimpahla ....

Summary

In order to express PLACE:

1. • **Most place names** (and certain special nouns) replace the initial vowel with **E-**
   eKapa, **e**Bhayi   (**e**khaya)
   • **Kwa-** is prefixed to Class 1a and 2a nouns and proper nouns to show the residence or property of ......
   kwaMazibuko, **kwa**Shell.

2. • Nouns in **Classes 1a and 2a** prefix **K-**
   kumama, **k**ooThemba

3. **All other nouns**
   • Replace the initial vowel with **E-**
   • Replace the final vowel as follows:

-a	→	-eni
-e	→	-eni
-i	→	-ini
-o	→	-weni
-u	→	-wini

Umsebenzi 7

Give the correct form of the noun in brackets and translate
1. Kukho iswekile (iti)?
2. Kukho amanzi (iketile)?
3. Qaba ibhotolo (isonka)!
4. Umama usebenza (ikhitshi)
5. Sityelela umhlobo (isibhedlele)

6. Khupha iimpahla (imoto)!
7. Simamela iindaba (umabonakude)
8. Ubhuti uvela (ooSipho)
9. Abantwana badlala (indlu)
10. Sifuna imisebenzi (uMzantsi Afrika)

Umsebenzi 8

Translate into Xhosa
1. Mother buys bread **at the shop**
2. Take the milk **out of the fridge**
3. The boys live **on a farm**
4. The girls are going **to grandmother** tomorrow
5. What do you see **in the picture**?
6. I am going **to town**
7. Father works **in the day** but **at night** he sleeps
8. Are you (plural) going **to the Smiths** tomorrow?
9. The children learn Xhosa **at school**
10. Beware of cars **on the roads**!

INCOKO

Abahlobo bayancokola.   *Friends are chatting.*

UDavid:	Uvela phi kanene Sipho?
USipho:	Ndivela **ema**Xhos**eni**. Wena, uvela phi?
UDavid:	Ndivela **e**Khimbali kodwa ndihlala apha **e**Kapa ngoku.
USipho:	Oo, uhlala ndawoni?
UDavid:	Ndihlala **e**Newlands. Wena, uhlala ndawoni **e**Kapa?
USipho:	Ndihlala **e**Gugulethu, **kwa**malume.
UDavid:	Usebenza phi?
USipho:	Ndisebenza **e**dolop**hini**, **kwa**Shell. Wena, uyasebenza?
UDavid:	Hayi, mna, ndisafunda **e**yunivesithi.
USipho:	Oo, ndiyabona. Uya phi ngoku?
UDavid:	Ndiya **e**zifund**weni**.
USipho:	Heke, hamba kakuhle mhlobo wam! Mna, ndiya **e**msebenz**ini**.
UDavid:	Nawe Sipho, hamba kakuhle!

Rewrite and practise this conversation using your personal particulars and those of a friend.

UMHOBE • A POEM

Utata uya phi?	Where is father going to?
Umama uya phi?	Where is mother going to?
Utat' uya **ebhankini,**	Father is going to the bank
Umam' uya **eposini,**	Mother is going to the post office,
Sisala **ekhaya!**	We remain at home!

UMHOBE • A POEM

Katana! Katana!	Kitten! Kitten!
Uya phi katana?	Where are you going to, kitten?
Ndiya **edolophini,**	I am going to town,
Ndiya kuthenga umnqwazi.	I am going to buy a hat.
Umnqwazi! Umnqwazi!	A hat! A hat!
Zange ndibone ikati	Never have I seen a cat
ithwele umnqwazi!	wearing a hat!
Njana! Njana!	Puppy! Puppy!
Uya phi njana?	Where are you going to, puppy
Ndiya **edolophini,**	I am going to town,
Ndiya kuthenga izihlangu.	I am going to buy shoes.
Izihlangu! Izihlangu!	Shoes! Shoes!
Zange ndibone inja	Never have I seen a dog
inxibe izihlangu!	wearing shoes!

NOTE

- The ending **-ana** denotes a diminutive.

ikati	→	ikat**ana**	kitten
inja	→	inj**ana**	puppy
umntu	→	umntw**ana**	child

- After the verb **-ya** (go to), the initial **u-** of **uku-** is dropped.
  Ndi**ya ku**thenga isonka   I am **going to** buy bread

- -thwala   wear on the head
  -nxiba   wear on other parts of the body
  ithwel**e**/inxib**e**   wear**ing**

INCOKO

OoMazibuko baya edolophini.   *The Mazibukos go to town.*

Umama: Khawulezisani bantwana! Nxibani! Siya **edolophini.**
Abantwana: Kulungile mama, siy<u>e</u>za.
               *Utata ukhupha imoto **egaraji.***
Utata: Khwelani! Siyahamba.
               *Umama <u>na</u>bantwana bakhwela **emotweni.***

Edolophini
Utata: Kulungile, mna ndiya **eofisini** ngoku.
Umama: Heke, mna ndifuna ukuya **ebhankini** kuqala. Ndifuna ukutsala
               imali. Emva koko ndiya **eposini.** Ndifuna ukuposa iileta
               <u>no</u>kuthenga izitampu.
Abantwana: Thina, sifuna iimpahla, mama.
UThemba: Mna, ndifuna ibhulukhwe <u>ne</u>hempe.
UNomsa: Mna, ndifuna ilokhwe <u>ne</u>zihlangu.
Umama: Kulungile, bantwana. Yiyani **evenkileni.** Ndiy<u>e</u>za.
               Lumkelani iimoto **ezindleleni!**

               Kamva: OoMazibuko bayagoduka. Badiniwe.

UNomsa ufuna
ilokhwe

Evenkileni

Izihlangu

UThemba ufuna
ibhulukhwe nehempe

Umsebenzi 9

Phendula imibuzo

1. OoMazibuko baya phi?
2. Utata ukhupha ntoni egaraji?
3. Oomama bakhwela ntoni?
4. Edolophini, utata uya phi?
5. Umama uya phi kuqala?
6. Emva koko uya phi?
7. Ufuna ukwenza ntoni apho?
8. Abantwana bafuna ntoni?
9. Nika isiNgesi: Lumkelani iimoto ezindleleni!
10. Nika isiXhosa: I am tired.

NOTE

-nika   give, hand to, supply with
-pha   give (as a gift)

Umsebenzi 10

Rewrite the following, filling in the blank spaces, and then read aloud.

OoMazibuko .....ya edolophini. Bakhwela .... *Utata* uya ....

Umama uya ebhankini .... Emva koko uya .... Uposa ....

Uthenga .... *Abantwana* bafuna ....

UThemba ufuna .... ne............... . *UNomsa* ufuna ....

ne............... . Kamva ba .... Ba............... .

Iimpahla zokunxiba • Clothes/Clothing
Literally 'goods of wearing'

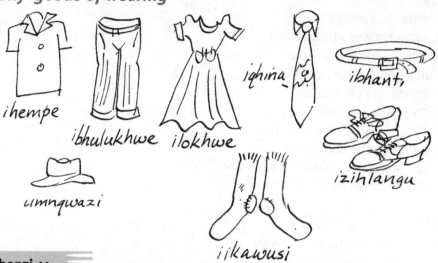

Umsebenzi 11

Complete the following table as indicated in the first line

Class	Singular	Plural	Meaning
3 & 4	**um**nqwazi	**imi**nqwazi	hat
	ibhulukhwe		
	ihempe		
	ilokhwe		
	isiketi		
	ijezi		
	ibhatyi		
	idyasi yemvula		
	ikawusi		
	isihlangu		
	iqhina		
	ibhanti		

Verbs associated with clothes:

-nxiba	wear, get dressed
-khulula	loosen, untie, undress
-hlamba	wash
-thenga	buy
-thunga	sew
-lungisa	make good, repair, mend, fix

Use these verbs to make some sentences of your own.

2. Expressing Time

Seasons of the year (Amaxesha onyaka)

ukwindla	→	**e**kwindla	**in** autumn
ubusika	→	**e**busika	**in** winter
intlakohlaza	→	**e**ntlakohlaza	**in** spring
ihlo<u>b</u>o	→	**e**hlo<u>ty</u>**eni**	**in** summer

Months of the year (Iinyanga zonyaka)

uJanuwari	uJulayi
uFebruwari	uAgasti
uMatshi	uSeptemba
uAprili	uOktobha
uMeyi	uNovemba
uJuni	uDisemba

NOTE

- **ngo**Januwari   **in** January
  nguJanuwari   **it is** January
- There are Xhosa words for the months but they are seldom used.

Days of the week (Iintsuku zeveki)

u**Mvulo**	Monday	(-vula	open)
uLwesi**bini**	Tuesday	(-bini	2)
uLwesi**thathu**	Wednesday	(-thathu	3)
uLwesi**ne**	Thursday	(-ne	4)
uLwesi**hlanu**	Friday	(-hlanu	5)
u**Mgqibelo**	Saturday	(-gqibela	finish)
iCawa	Sunday	(icawa	church)

- **ngo**Mvulo **on** Monday
  nguMvulo **it is** Monday $\Big\}$ (for all days except **Sunday**)
- **nge**Cawa **on** Sunday
  yiCawa **it is** Sunday

Times of the Day (Amaxesha emini)

emini	**in** the day
ebusuku	**at** night
kusasa	in the morning
emva kwemini/emalanga	in the afternoon
ngokuhlwa	in the evening

Hours of the Day (Iiyure zemini)

Generally, the English numerals are used to tell the time of day, the Xhosa numbers being long and complicated.

NOTE

- **Nga**bani ixesha? **At** what time?
  Nini? When?
  Ngo6 **At** 6 o'clock

- **Ngu**bani ixesha? What **is** the time?
  Ngu2.15 **It is** 2.15

  Study the following examples
  Uhamba **ngabani** ixesha? Ndihamba **ngo**8
  Ibhasi ifika **nini**? Ifika **ngo**8.30
  Ngubani ixesha? **Ngu**12.20

Other useful words relating to time

namhlanje	today
izolo	yesterday
ngomso	tomorrow
ngenye imini	one day
yonke imihla	every day
imini yonke	the whole day
kule veki	(in) this week

kule nyanga	(in) this month
kulo (m)nyaka	(in) this year
evek**ini**	**in** the week
ngempelaveki	**in** the weekend

N o t e

3 & 4	**um**nyaka	**imi**nyaka	year
The **m** in **um**nyaka may be omitted		→	**u**nyaka

Umsebenzi 12

Translate into English
1. Kuyabanda **ebusika** kodwa kushushu **ehlotyeni**.
2. Kumnandi **ekwindla** kodwa umoya uvuthuza kakhulu **entlakohlaza**.
3. Izikolo zivala **ngo**Disemba **nango**Januwari.
4. **Ngo**Mvulo, **ngo**Lwesibini, **ngo**Lwesithathu, **ngo**Lwesine **nango**Lwesihlanu siyasebenza.
5. **Ngo**Mgqibelo siya edolophini. Abantwana bahlala **ekhaya**.
6. **Nge**Cawa siya ecaweni.
7. Abantwana bayafunda **kusasa**. Badlala imidlalo **emva kwemini**.
8. Utata ufika ekhaya **ngo**6 **ngokuhlwa**.
9. Uxolo! **Ngu**bani ixesha, nkosikazi? **Ngu**5.10.
10. Ndizama ukuthetha isiXhosa **yonke imihla**!

3. Counting (Ukubala)

As mentioned earlier, the Xhosa numbers are complicated. In the case of counting, the verb link (in front of the number) will also vary according to what is being counted. For example:

Abantu **ba**bini	The people are two
Iimoto **zim**bini	The cars are two
or	
Abantu **aba**bini	Two people
Iimoto **ezim**bini	Two cars

inye..zimbini..zintathu

75

1. -nye
2. -bini
3. -thathu
4. -ne
5. -hlanu
6. -thandathu
7. **isi**xhenxe   } Class 7
8. **isi**bhozo
9. **i**thoba   } Class 5
10. **i**shumi

NOTE

- The numbers 1 to 6 are adjective stems
  The numbers 7 to 10 are nouns.
- **Uyakwazi ukubala?**
  Ewe, ndiyakwazi!
  Mamela ... 1 – 10
  Do you know how to count?
  Yes, I do know how to!
  Listen ... 1 – 10

Uyakwazi ukubala?   *Ewe ndiyakwazi!*
                          Mamela ...

ISIGAMA

Nouns

Class		
7	**isi**bhedlele	hospital
9	**i**khemesti	chemist
9	**i**fama	farm
9	**i**yunivesithi	university
–	**u**lwandle	sea
9	**i**mini	day, daytime
–	**ubu**suku	night
1a	**u**nomathotholo	radio
–	**u**ncedo	help
9	**in**taba	mountain
9	**i**tafile	table
9	**i**gadi	garden
9	**i**bhanki	bank
9	**i**posi	post, post office
9	**i**ketile	kettle

5	**i**gumbi	room
1	**um**hlobo	friend
9	**in**dlela	road, way
5	**i**langa	sun
9	**i**bhedi	bed
9	**in**tolongo	prison, jail
9	**in**taka	bird
5	**i**yeza	medicine
9	**i**bhotolo	butter
5	**i**khitshi	kitchen
1a	**u**mabonakude	television set
9	**i**friji	fridge
9	**in**dawo	place, locality
1a	**u**malume	uncle (maternal)
9	**i**ofisi	office
9	**i**leta	letter
10	**iim**pahla zokunxiba	clothes, clothing
3	**um**nqwazi	hat
9	**i**bhulukhwe	trousers (pair of)
9	**i**hempe	shirt
9	**i**lokhwe	dress
7	**isi**hlangu	shoe
7	**isi**keti	skirt
9	**i**jezi	jersey
9	**i**bhatyi	jacket
9	**i**dyasi yemvula	raincoat
9	**i**kawusi	sock
5	**i**qhina	tie
9	**i**bhanti	belt
3	**u(m)**nyaka	year
9	**in**yanga	month, moon
9	**i**veki	week
–	**u**suku/**iin**tsuku	24-hour day
9	**i**yure	hour
–	**ukw**indla	autumn
–	**ubu**sika	winter
9	**in**tlakohlaza	spring
5	**i**hlobo	summer
9	**i**cawa	church
9	**im**pelaveki	weekend
3	**um**dlalo	game

Verbs

-bhala	write
-beka	put, place
-lala	lie down, sleep
-khwela	ride, get on
-tsala	pull, withdraw
-qaba	spread
-tyelela	visit
-lumkela	beware of
-ncokola	chat
-thwala	bear, carry
-nxiba	wear, get dressed
-posa	post
-nika	give
-pha	give
-khulula	loosen, undress
-thunga	sew
-lungisa	repair, mend
-gqiba	finish (doing something)
-gqibela	finish for, finish off
-banda	be cold (things)
-zama	try, strive
-bala	count

General

e**Pitoli**	**to** Pretoria
e**Khimbali**	**from** Kimberley
e**Melika**	**from** America
e**Ngilani**	**in** England
abantu aba**ninzi**	**many** people
kanene	by the way
ndaw**oni**?	at **what** place?
mna/**we**na	as for **me**/as for **you**
heke!	good! well done!
nam/**na**we	me **too**/you (singular) **too**
na-/ne-/no-	and
kuqala	firstly
thina	as for us
kamva	afterwards, later
badiniwe	they are tired

78

apho	there
kusasa	in the morning
emva kwemini ⎱ emalanga	in the afternoon
ngokuhlwa	in the evening
izolo	yesterday
ngenye imini	one day
yonke imihla	every day
imini yonke	the whole day
kule veki	in this week
kule nyanga	in this month
kulo (m)nyaka	in this year
evek**ini**	**in** the week
ngempelaveki	**in** the weekend
kuyabanda	**it is** cold
kushushu	**it is** hot
kumnandi	**it is** nice/pleasant
Uya**kw**azi **uku**...?	Can you ...?/Do you know how to...?
Ewe, ndiya**kw**azi	Yes, I can
Hayi, andi**kw**azi	No, I can't

NOTE

For **months** of the year and **days** of the week, see page 73.

Na- and Nga- • Absolute Pronouns

1. Na- and Nga-

Both **Na-** and **Nga-** have several meanings and are used a great deal.

Na-
- **and** (joining nouns)
- **with** (together with)
- **have**

Nga-
- **with/by** (by means of)
- **about** (concerning)
- to indicate **time** and **place**

Note
- The **a** of **na-** and **nga-** combines with the initial vowel of the noun with which it is used, as follows:

a + a → a	**na**manzi	**and** water
a + i → e	**ne**kofu	**and** coffee
a + u → o	**no**tata	**and** father

- Nouns begin with the vowels **a**, **i** or **u**.

- Class 2a: **a + oo**   →   **oo**
  Class 10:   **a + ii**   →   **ee**

Three uses of Na-

1. Na-   And (joining nouns)

Study the following examples

na- + **a**manzi	→	**na**manzi	**and** water
na- + **i**kofu	→	**ne**kofu	**and** coffee
na- + **u**tata	→	**no**tata	**and** father

Khangela ioyile **na**manzi	Check the oil **and** water
Kukho iti **ne**kofu	There is tea **and** coffee
Ndibulisa umama **no**tata	I greet mother **and** father

NOTE

Na- (and) can be translated as **also/too**

NoMary ufuna ukuhamba	**And** Mary/Mary **too** wants to go

Umsebenzi 1

Join the following nouns using na- (and) and translate

1. isonka + **a**manzi
2. isonka + **i**bhotolo
3. isonka + **u**bisi
4. umntwana + **a**bazali
5. ioyile + **i**bhetri
6. uNomsa + **u**Themba
7. intombazana + **i**nkwenkwe
8. amantombazana + **a**makhwenkwe
9. izihlangu + **u**mnqwazi
10. isiXhosa + **i**siAfrikansi

Umsebenzi 2

Join the following nouns using na- (and) and translate

1. oobhuti + **oo**sisi
2. izinja + **ii**kati
3. iimela + **ii**folokhwe
4. oomama + **oo**tata
5. izihlangu + **ii**kawusi

Umsebenzi 3

Translate the following nouns and join, using na- (and)

1. time + money
2. bank + post office
3. man + woman
4. men + women
5. fire + wind
6. trousers + shirt
7. door + windows
8. knives + spoons
9. brother + Sipho and others
10. money + power

UMDLALO • A GAME

Together with a partner, practise using **na-** to join two nouns. The nouns may be given in:

- Xhosa (where **sound** is important, **na-**, **ne-** or **no-**)
- English (to improve **vocabulary**)

Once the use of **na-**, **ne-** and **no-** becomes more familiar, a verb should be introduced to make the example more meaningful.

Ndifuna imela + ifolokhwe	→	Ndifuna imela **ne**folokhwe.
Galela iswekile + ubisi	→	Galela iswekile **no**bisi.
Thenga isonka + amaqanda	→	Thenga isonka **na**maqanda.

NOTE

Study the following examples

- UThemba noSipho **ba**yasebenza   Themba and Sipho (they) are working
- Inja nekati **zi**yalwa   The dog and the cat (they) are fighting
- Amadoda namakhwenkwe **a**yafika   The men and the boys (they) are arriving

Generally, the verb link for **people** is **ba-** and for **animals/things** it is **zi-**.
However, if the two nouns are in the same class, the verb link of that class is used. Otherwise use the link of the noun closest to the verb.

Umsebenzi 4

Fill in the correct verb link and translate

1. Umama notata ..... yaphangela
2. Iteksi nebhasi ..... fika ngo8 kusasa
3. Inja nekati .... dlala ngaphandle
4. Amadoda nabafazi ..... sebenza efama
5. Amakhwenkwe namantombazana ..... yadlala

NOTE

- **Na-** (and) cannot be used to join verbs.
  I get up, **and** get dressed   Ndiyavuka, ndinxib**e**
  This is altogether a different construction and will not be dealt with.

- However, **na-** (and) may be used with the infinitive **uku-**
  I like to work **and** to play   Ndithanda ukusebenza **no**kudlala

Umsebenzi 5

Translate into Xhosa
1. We are learning to write **and to** speak Xhosa
2. People like to eat **and to** drink
3. Children like to play **and to** run
4. In the weekend we like to rest **and to** sleep
5. I know how (can) to speak **and to** read Xhosa

2. Na-   (together) **With**

Study the following examples

Ndithetha **na**bahlobo	I talk **with/to** friends
Ndidlala **ne**nja	I play **with** the dog
Ndisebenza **no**Zodwa	I work **with** Zodwa

Umsebenzi 6

Complete the following sentences using na- (with) and translate
1. Ndifuna ukuthetha ..... (uThandi)
2. Abantwana bagoduka ..... (abazali)
3. Indoda ihamba entabeni ..... (inja)
4. ULizo usebenza ..... (utata)
5. Amantombazana adlala ..... (amakhwenkwe)

NOTE

- **Na-** (with) may be used with **bani** (who)

Ndithetha **na**bani?	**With** whom am I speaking?
Uhlala **na**bani?	**With** whom do you live/stay?

- Class 2a: Ndithetha **noo**Themba   I am speaking **to** Themba and others
  Class 10: Ndithetha **nee**ntombi   I am speaking **to** the girls

Umsebenzi 7

Answer the following questions using the noun in brackets and translate
1. Uncokola **na**bani? (uJenny)
2. UZodwa uhlala **na**bani? (umhlobo)
3. Abantwana badlala **na**bani? (abahlobo)
4. Ufuna ukuthetha **na**bani? (uNomsa)
5. Ubhuti usebenza **noo**bani? (uThemba noLizo)

3. -na-   Have

Study the following examples

Ndi**na**bantwana	I **have** children
Ndi**ne**moto	I **have** a car
Ndi**no**mhlobo	I **have** a friend

N O T E

- **-na-** does not stand on its own.
- There is no **-ya-**!
- Class 2a   U**noo**bhuti?   Do you have brothers?
  Class 10   U**nee**lekese?   Do you have sweets?

Umsebenzi 8

Use the following nouns as indicated in the example

imali   Ndi**ne**mali   I have money

1. umntwana
2. abantwana
3. inja
4. iikati
5. umsebenzi

6. indlu
7. abahlobo
8. izitampu
9. ubisi
10. iphephandaba

Umsebenzi 9

Use the following nouns as indicated in the example

ibhayisekile   U**ne**bhayisekile?   Ewe, ndi**ne**bhayisekile.

1. umsebenzi
2. ixesha
3. amatikiti
4. umpu
5. iincwadi

Study the following examples

UThemba **u**nebhayisekile	Themba **(he)** has a bicycle
Abantwana **ba**neebhayisekile	The children **(they)** have bicycles
Intombi **i**nebhayisekile	The girl **(she)** has a bicycle

N O T E

The verb link comes immediately before **-na-** (have).

84

Umsebenzi 10

Complete the following using the correct verb link with -na- (have) and translate

1. Indoda .... (imoto)
2. UMary .... (umntwana)
3. Iintombi .... (abahlobo)
4. Utata .... (ifama)
5. Abamelwane .... (izinja)

Umsebenzi 11

Answer the following questions as shown in the example
UThemba **une**moto?
Ewe, **une**moto   Yes, he **has** a car

1. Umntwana **una**bazali?
2. Abafundi ba**nee**ncwadi?
3. Indoda **ino**msebenzi?
4. Abantwana ba**ne**zihlangu?
5. Wena, **une**bhatyi?

NOTE

-na- (have) may be used with **ntoni** (what) as follows:
Unantoni?   Lit: What do you **have?**/What have you **got?**
               What is troubling you?/What is wrong with you?

Unantoni?	What is wrong with you?
Ndi**ne**ntloko	I **have** a head(ache)
Ndi**ne**sisu	I **have** a stomach(ache)
Ndi**ne**sifuba	I **have** a (bad) chest
Ndi**ne**fiva	I **have** a fever

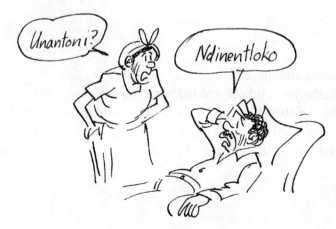

Umsebenzi 12

Answer the following questions using the noun in brackets and translate
1. Unantoni? (intloko)
2. Umntwana unantoni? (isifuba)
3. Intombi inantoni? (umona)
4. UThemba unantoni? (isithuthuthu)
5. Umfana unantoni? (ingxaki)

NOTE

The following expressions use **-na-** (have)
- Uneminyaka emingaphi?   You **have** how many years?
  How old are you?
- Unabantwana abangaphi? You **have** how many children?
  How many children do you have?

-ngaphi? (how many) is an adjective and thus has its own set of links.
Merely use the English numerals in replying.

UMDLALO • A GAME

The same game played with na- (and) may be played with -na- (have).
- One person should give a Xhosa noun such as **ikati** to which the other
  would reply **Ndinekati**.

- Two Xhosa nouns such as **umntwana + ikati**, should be given, and the
  other should reply **Umntwana unekati.**

Umsebenzi 13

Complete the following using na- and translate into English
na-   and
na-   (together) **with**
-na-   have

1. Abazali .... (abantwana) bayeza
2. Ndiyakwazi ukuthetha ... (ukubhala) isiXhosa
3. USipho uthetha ... (intombi)
4. UNomsa u- ..... (intloko)
5. Ndi- ..... (ingxaki)

NOTE

The following idiomatic expressions use -na- (have).

1. Unentloko   He has a head
                He is clever
2. Uneliso   He has an eye
                He has an expert eye for ...
3. Unomlomo   He has a mouth
                He talks too much
4. Unolwimi   He has a tongue
                He is a bearer of tales/He gossips
5. Unesandla   He has a hand
                He is an expert at a particular craft

Three uses of Nga-

1. Nga-   With/By (by means of)

Study the following examples

Ndihlamba **nga**manzi	(nga + amanzi)	I wash **with** water
Ndibhala **nge**pensile	(nga + ipensile)	I write **with** a pencil
Ndihamba **ngo**loliwe	(nga + uloliwe)	I go/travel **by** train

Umsebenzi 14

Complete the following using nga- (with/by) and translate

1. Sitya ..... (imela) nefolokhwe
2. Sihlamba ..... (amanzi) nesepha
3. Umfana uhamba ..... (imoto) okanye ..... (uloliwe)
4. Abantwana bahamba .....(iinyawo)
5. Indoda ibamba utata ..... (isandla) i.e. shakes hands
6. Sithenga iimpahla ..... (imali)
7. Ukhetha ukubhala ..... (ipensile) okanye ..... (usiba)?
8. Abantwana bathanda ukutya ..... (izandla)
9. Sika isonka ..... (imela)!
10. Zalisa iketile ..... (amanzi)!

NOTE

Nga- (with/by) may be used with **ntoni** (what).

Uhamba **nga**ntoni?	Ndihamba **nge**moto
Uhlawula **nga**ntoni?	Ndihlawula **nge**khadi
Ubhala **nga**ntoni?	Ndibhala **nge**pensile

NOTE

Ukuhamba	To go or travel
ngemoto	**by** car
ngebhasi	**by** bus
ngeteksi	**by** taxi
ngebhayisekile	**by** bicycle
ngesithuthuthu	**by** motorbike
ngetreyini/**ngo**loliwe	**by** train
ngenqwelomoya	**by** aeroplane
ngenqanawa	**by** ship
ngeenyawo	**by/on** foot

Umsebenzi 15

Answer the following questions using the noun in brackets and translate

1. UPeter uhamba **nga**ntoni ukuya emsebenzini? (isithuthuthu)
2. Abantwana baya esikolweni **nga**ntoni? (iinyawo)
3. Umfazi ubhatala **nga**ntoni? (itsheki)
4. Ubhala **nga**ntoni? (usiba)
5. Abafana bathanda ukuhamba **nga**ntoni? (iiteksi)

NOTE

- Uhamba **nga**ntoni ukuya emsebenzini?
  Uya emsebenzini **nga**ntoni? } How do you go to work?

- Uhlawula/Ubhatala **nga**ntoni?

ngekhadi	**by** card
ngetsheki	**by** cheque
ngekheshi	**by** cash
Thenga **nge**akhawunti	Buy **on** account

Learn the following

- Uthini **nge**siXhosa? — What do you say **in** Xhosa?
  Yintoni le **nge**siXhosa? — What is this **in** Xhosa?
  Ngubani igama lakho **nge**siXhosa? — What is your name **in** Xhosa?

- Sibhatala **nge**mini — We pay **by** the day
  Sibhatala **nge**veki — We pay **by** the week
  Sibhatala **nge**nyanga — We pay **by** the month

- Galela ipetroli **nge**R50 — Pour in petrol **with** R50 (worth)
  Mpompa amavili **nge** 2 bar — Pump the wheels **with** 2 bars
- Funda **nge**ntloko — Learn **by** heart (lit: by head)
- Hamba **ngo**xolo — Go **in** peace
- **nga + noun**

nga- + **a**mandla	→	**nga**mandla	strongly, fast
nga- + **i**siqhelo	→	**nge**siqhelo	usually
nga- + **i**lishwa	→	**nge**lishwa	unfortunately
nga- + **i**thamsanqa	→	**nge**thamsanqa	fortunately
nga- + **u**kukhawuleza	→	**ngo**kukhawuleza	quickly

2. Nga-   About (concerning)

Study the following examples

Ndithetha **nga**bamelwane — I am talking **about** the neighbours
Ndithetha **nge**ntombi — I am talking **about** the girl
Ndithetha **ngo**Lindiwe — I am talking **about** Lindiwe

Umsebenzi 16

Complete using nga- (about), and translate
1. Umfazi ubuza (utata)
2. OoNono bathetha (isikolo)
3. ULindile ubhala (iholide) efama
4. Abantwana bafunda (iinyoka) esikolweni
5. Iintombi zincokola (abafana)

NOTE

- **nga-** (about) may be used with **ntoni** (what) and **bani** (who).
  Uthetha **nga**ntoni? — What are you talking **about**?
  Uthetha **nga**bani? — Whom are you talking **about**?

- Ndixelele **nga** ... — Tell me **about** ....
  Ndixelele **nge**holide — Tell me **about** the holiday

- Enkosi **nga** .... — Thank you **for** ...
  Enkosi **nge**sipho — Thank you **for** the gift

Answer the question and translate
1. Ititshala ithetha **nga**bani? (uLizo)
2. Umfana ubuza **nga**ntoni? (ingozi)

*Complete the statement using **nga-** (about) and translate*
3. Ndixelele (umsebenzi) wakho
4. Enkosi kakhulu (uncedo)
5. Enkosi kakhulu (imali)

3. Nga-   To indicate **Time** and **Place**

Note the following examples

Time

ngabani ixesha?	**at** what time?
ngo 10	**at** 10 o'clock
ngoMvulo	**on** Monday
ngoJanuwari	**in** January
ngo1994	**in** 1994
ngokuhlwa	**in** the evening
ngempelaveki	**in** the weekend

Place

ngaphandle	outside
ngaphakathi	inside
ngaseKapa	in the vicinity of Cape Town
ngaselwandle	near the sea
ngapha	**in** this direction

-NGA-   To indicate **May/Can** (permission)

Ndi**nga**ngena?	**May** I come in?
Ndi**nga**thetha noMary?	**May** I speak to Mary?
Ndi**nga**kunceda?	**Can** I help <u>you</u>?
U**nga**hamba ukuba uyafuna.	You **may** go if you want to.

- It is clear from the above examples that **-nga-** (may/can) is used differently from the other **nga-**.

- **-ya-** is not used with **-nga-**.

Listen to the following passage and then read aloud several times, before answering the questions.

UNomsa uhamba **nge**teksi.   Nomsa travels **by** taxi.

UNomsa uya emsebenzini **nge**teksi. Uthi uthanda ukuncokola **na**bantu eteksini. Bancokola **ngo**msebenzi, **nge**khaya **nanga**bahlobo. UNomsa uya<u>ba</u>xelela ukuba ufunda ukuthetha **no**kubhala isiNgesi emsebenzini. **Ngo**5:30 **ngo**kuhlwa ugoduka **na**bahlobo kwakhona.
UThemba, yena, u**ne**sithuthuthu. Uthi ukhetha ukuhamba **nge**sithuthuthu kuba siyakhawuleza.
Abantwana, bona, bahamba **ngee**nyawo ukuya esikolweni.

Abantwana bahamba ngeenyawo

UThemba uhamba ngesithuthuthu

UNomsa uhamba ngeteksi

Isigama

uya<u>ba</u>xelela	she tells <u>them</u>	yena	as for him
ukuba	that	bona	as for them
kuba	because		

Umsebenzi 18

Phendula imibuzo

1. UNomsa uya **nga**ntoni emsebenzini?
2. Uthanda ukwenza ntoni eteksini?
3. Bancokola **nga**ntoni?
4. UNomsa ufunda ntoni emsebenzini?
5. Bagoduka **nga**bani ixesha?
6. UThemba, yena, u**na**ntoni?
7. Uthi ukhetha ukuhamba **nge**sithuthuthu. Kutheni? (... kuba...)
8. Abantwana, bona, bahamba **nga**ntoni ukuya esikolweni?
9. Wena, uyakwazi ukukhwela isithuthuthu?
10. Wena, uhamba **nga**ntoni ukuya emsebenzini?

2. Absolute Pronouns

Person	Absolute Pronoun	Noun	Verb
1st	**Mna**		**ndi**yasebenza
	Thina		**si**yafunda
2nd	**Wena**		uyahamba
	Nina		**ni**yasala
3rd (Classes)			
1	**Yena**	**um**fazi	uyathunga
2	**Bona**	**aba**fazi	**ba**yapheka
1a	**Yena**	**u**Thandi	uyazama
2a	**Bona**	**oo**Thandi	**ba**yancokola
9	**Yona**	**in**ja	iyaluma
10	**Zona**	**izin**ja	**zi**yakhonkotha

N O T E

- The absolute pronoun translates **as for me, as for you**, etc.
  It emphasises the verb link.
- It can be used with or without the noun.
  UThemba **yena** uyahamba
  Yena uyahamba
- It can stand on its own, unlike the verb link, and may come before or after
  the noun.
  Yena umfazi or Umfazi **yena**
- Each class has its own absolute pronoun.
  Those used most frequently are given in the table.
  Classes 1 and 1a   **yena** } generally people
  Classes 2 and 2a   **bona** }
  Class 9   **yona** } generally things or animals
  Class 10   **zona** }

Umsebenzi 19

Fill in the correct absolute pronoun and translate
1. Ubhuti .... uyahleka
2. Abantwana .... bayangxola
3. Umntwana .... uyaxoka
4. OoMandisa .... bacela isitshixo
5. Intombi .... iyalila
6. Iintombi .... ziyaphumla

7. Itreyini .... iyafika
8. Iitreyini .... zifika kade namhlanje
9. Uyise .... usebenza edolophini
10. Abamelwane .... bayafuduka

Umsebenzi 20

Fill in the missing absolute pronoun and then listen to the dialogue.

ULindi: Molo Thandi! Kunjani?

UThandi: Molo Lindi! Ndiphilile. .... unjani?

ULindi: Hayi, ... ndisaphila, enkosi. Umyeni wakho .... unjani?

UThandi: Hayi, uphilile.

ULindi: Abantwana .... banjani?

UThandi: Hayi, baphilile. .... ninjani ekhaya?

ULindi: Hayi, ... siphilile, enkosi.

The absolute pronouns for Classes 3 to 8 are:

Class	Absolute Pronoun	Noun	Meaning
3	**wona**	**um**thetho	**as for it**, the law
4	**yona**	**imi**thetho	**as for them**, the laws
5	**lona**	**i**yeza	**as for it**, the medicine
6	**wona**	**ama**yeza	**as for them**, the medicines
7	**sona**	**isi**tshixo	**as for it**, the key
8	**zona**	**izi**tshixo	**as for them**, the keys

The absolute pronoun used with na- and nga-

Study the following examples

UThemba na**m**	Themba and **I**
Ndifuna ukuhamba na**we**	I want to go with **you**
Sina**yo** (imoto)	We have **it/one** (a car)
Sihamba nga**yo** (imoto)	We travel by **it** (car)
Ndithetha nga**ye** (uNomsa)	I am talking about **her** (Nomsa)
Ndithetha nga**bo** (ooNomsa)	I am talking about **them** (Nomsa and others)

NOTE

Ku- (to, from, with) can also be used as above.

Yiza ku**m**!	Come to **me**!
Kunjani ku**we**?	How is it with **you**?
Isipho sivela ku**ye** (umama)	The gift comes from **her** (mother)
Isipho sivela ku**bo** (abazali)	The gift comes from **them** (parents)
Ndiya ku**yo** (indlu)	I am going to **it** (the house)

NB Thus when **na-**, **nga-** or **ku-** is prefixed to the absolute pronoun, the final **-na** is dropped.

Umsebenzi 21

Translate
1. Ufuna ukuthetha **nam**?
2. Ewe, ndifuna ukuthetha **nawe**
3. **Nam**, ndiyeza
4. **Nathi**, siyaphila
5. Sithetha **ngaye**
6. Ileta ivela **kubo**
7. Unemali? Ewe, **ndinayo**
8. Ninabantwana? Ewe, **sinabo**
9. Uhamba **nge**nqwelomoya? Ewe, ndihamba **ngayo**
10. Si**nga**dibana **nani** ngomso?

NOTE

Some verbs are followed by na-
-dibana	+ na-	meet (with)
-fana	+ na-	be similar (to)
-tshata	+ na-	marry (to/with)

Umsebenzi 22

Give the correct form of the word in brackets and translate
1. Ndifuna ukudibana (wena) ngomso.
2. Umntwana ufana (uyise). Ufana (yena)
3. ULizo utshata (uMandisa). Utshata (yena)
4. UThandi udibana (abahlobo). Udibana (bona)
5. Intombi ifana (unina). Ifana (yena)

INCOKO
*UThandi udibana **na**bahlobo.*   *Thandi meets **with** friends.*

UThandi:	Molweni!
Abahlobo:	Molo Thandi!
UThandi:	Ninjani?
Abahlobo:	Sikhona, enkosi. Kunjani **ku**we?
UThandi:	Kulungile, enkosi. Nincokola **nga**ntoni?
Abahlobo:	**Nga**bantwana, **ngo**msebenzi, **nge**mali, njalo njalo.

UThandi:	Oo ndiyabona. Ndi**nga**hlala phantsi?
Abahlobo:	Ewe, hlal' apha Thandi!
	(*UThandi uhlala phantsi nabahlobo*)
Abahlobo:	Wena, u**na**bantwana Thandi?
UThandi:	Ewe, ndi**na**bo.
Abahlobo:	Bangaphi?
UThandi:	Babini – inkwenkwe **ne**ntombi. Bona, bayafunda.
Abahlobo:	Bahamba **nga**ntoni ukuya esikolweni?
UThandi:	Bahamba **nge**enyawo.
Abahlobo:	Wena, uyaphangela?
UThandi:	Ewe, ndiyafundisa.
Abahlobo:	Uya **nga**ntoni emsebenzini?
UThandi:	Ndihamba **nge**teksi okanye **nge**bhasi.
Abahlobo:	Nina, ni**ne**moto?
Uthandi:	Ewe, si**na**yo kodwa ipetroli idulu! Umyeni wam, yena, uhamba **nga**yo.
Abahlobo:	Yinyaniso! **Na**thi sikhalaza **nge**mali. Yonke into idulu namhlanje. Si**nga**thini?
UThandi:	Yho! Ixesha limkile! Abantwana babuya esikolweni **ngo**2.
Abahlobo:	Uhambe kakuhle Thandi!
UThandi:	Nisale kakuhle nina!

NOTE

- bayafunda   they are studying, that is, they are (still) 'at school'
- Uhamb**e** kakuhle!   You (singular) should go well
  Nisal**e** kakuhle!   You (plural) should stay well
  This form of saying goodbye is used a great deal.

Umsebenzi 23

Listen carefully to the passage about Thandi (in Xhosa) before translating.

Thandi greets her friends. They are chatting. They are chatting **about** children, **about** work, **about** money, etc. She sits down **with** them. They ask questions. Thandi answers. She says she **has** children – a boy **and** a girl. As for them, they are at school (they are studying). They go to school **on** foot. Thandi, as for her, she teaches. She goes to work **by** taxi or **by** bus. (Her) husband, as for him, he travels **by** car, but petrol is expensive. The friends, they **too**, are complaining **about** money. Everything is expensive today. What **can** we do? Thandi goes home because it is late. The children return from school **at** 2 o'clock. She says goodbye (she greets).

INCOKO

Efonini   *On the telephone*
Ifoni iyakhala

Inkosikazi:	Hullo!
UThemba:	Hullo! Ndi**nga**thetha noLizo?
Inkosikazi:	Ndilusizi, akakho.
UThemba:	Ubuya nini?
Inkosikazi:	**Ngo**2 emva kwemini.
UThemba:	Kulungile. Ndi**nga**shiya umyalezo?
Inkosikazi:	Ewe, ngokuqinisekileyo.
UThemba:	NdinguThemba Majola. ULizo u**na**yo inamba yam. A**nga**ndifonela ngokuhlwa ekhaya okanye ngomso emsebenzini.
Inkosikazi:	Kulungile, ndizomnika umyalezo.
UThemba:	Enkosi. Ndithetha **na**bani?
Inkosikazi:	Inkosikazi yakhe.
UThemba:	Ndiyabulela, nkosikazi. Bhabhayi.
Inkosikazi:	Bhabhayi!

NB
Uxolo!   Sorry/Excuse me/I beg your pardon **(apology)**
Ndilusizi!   I am sad/sorry **(sympathy)**

Phendula le mibuzo

1. UThemba ufuna ukuthetha nabani?
2. Ukhona?
3. Ubuya nini?
4. UThemba ucela ukwenza ntoni?
5. ULizo unayo inamba **ka**Themba **(of)**?
6. UThemba uthetha nabani efonini?

Nika isiXhosa

7. May I speak to Vuyani?
8. Certainly!
9. To whom am I speaking?
10. I am grateful

Now try to write your own telephone conversation.

Useful phrases for the telephone:

Ndi**nga**thetha noThandi?	**May** I speak to Thandi?
Ndicela ukuthetha **no**Thandi?	I request to speak **to** Thandi
UThandi u**khona**?	Is Thandi **there**?
Ewe, u**khona**!	Yes, **he/she** is here!
Hayi, **aka**kho!	No, **he/she** is not here!
Bamba nje	Just hold
Ndizo**m**biza	I'll call **him/her**
Ndithetha **na**bani?	**To** whom am I speaking?
NguThemba othethayo	**It is** Themba who is speaking
Khawu**m**nike umyalezo	Please give **him/her** a message
Nantsi inamba yam	**Here is** my number
Ndiyabulela	I am grateful

ISIGAMA

Nouns

Class

9	**i**mela	knife
9	**i**folokhwe	fork
5	**i**cephe	spoon
9	**i**teksi	taxi
9	**i**bhayisekile	bicycle
9	**i**fiva	fever

3	**um**ona	jealousy
7	**isi**thuthuthu	mtorbike
9	**in**gxaki	problem
9	**i**pensile	pencil
–	**u**siba	pen, feather
9	**i**sepha	soap
1a	**u**loliwe	train
9	**i**treyini	train
9	**in**qwelomoya	aeroplane
9	**in**qanawa	ship
9	**i**tsheki	cheque
9	**i**kheshi	cash
9	**i**akhawunti	account
–	**u**xolo	peace
7	**isi**qhelo	habit
5	**ili**shwa	misfortune
5	**i**thamsanqa	good fortune, luck
–	**uku**khawuleza	hurrying
1	**um**melwane	neighbour
9	**i**holide	holiday
9	**in**yoka	snake
–	**uku**hlwa	evening
1	**um**yeni	husband
1a	**u**yise	his/her/their father
1a	**u**nina	his/her/their mother
9	**in**yaniso	truth
9	**i**foni	telephone
–	**u**sizi	pity
3	**um**yalezo	message
9	**i**namba	number

Verbs

-lwa	fight
-phumla	rest
-bamba	hold, catch, arrest
-khetha	prefer, choose
-sika	cut
-hlawula ⎫ -bhatala ⎭	pay
-xela	tell

-xelela	tell to
-khonkotha	bark
-fuduka	move house
-dibana + na-	meet (with)
-fana + na-	be similar (to)
-tshata + na-	marry (to/with)
-fundisa	teach
-khalaza	complain
-buya	return from
-buyela	return to
-khala	cry out, scream
-shiya	leave (behind)
-fona	phone
-fonela	phone to
-bulela	be grateful

General

-ngaphi?	how many? (adjective)
le	this/these (Class 9/4 nouns)
ngamandla	strongly, fast
ngesiqhelo	usually
ngelishwa	unfortunately
ngethamsanqa	fortunately, luckily
ngokukhawuleza	quickly
ukuba	if; that
kwakhona	again
yena	as for **him/her/it**
bona	as for **them**
kuba	because
njalo njalo	etc. etc.
yinyaniso	**it is** the truth
singathi**ni**?	**what** can we say/do?
ixesha limk**ile**	the time **has** departed (it's late)
ndilusizi	I am sad/sorry
ukhona?	**is he/she** present/here/there?
akakho	**he/she is not** present/here/there
ngokuqinisekileyo	certainly
anga**ndi**fonela	he can phone **me**
okanye	or
ndizo**m**nika	I'll give **him**
bhabhayi	bye-bye

8 Noun Classes 11, 14 & 15 •
Verb Links with other Parts of Speech

1. Noun Classes 11, 14 & 15

Study the following examples

Ndifuna	**ulu**thi	I want a stick
Ndithanda	**ubu**si	I like honey
Ndithenga	**uku**tya	I buy food

- The last three classes (11, 14 & 15) form a unit at the end of the list of noun classes. They can be referred to as the **ulu- ubu- uku-** classes, according to their prefixes.
- Notice that there are no Classes 12 and 13 in Xhosa. But, because all African or
  * Bantu languages have the same class system, the numbers 12 and 13 are left intact to allow for comparison.
  * A linguistic term for a large group of languages spoken in Africa.

Classes 11 & 10

Prefixes: ulu-/u- & izin-/iin-

Class 11 (singular)   **Class 10** (plural)

Stems of one syllable or sound

Class 11	Class 10	
uluthi	**izin**ti	stick
uluvo	**izim**vo	opinions
uluntu	–	community
ulutsha	–	youth

uluthi

Stems of more than one syllable or sound

Class 11	Class 10	
unyawo	**iin**yawo	foot
unwele	**iin**wele	hair
uzwane	**iin**zwane	toe
udonga	**iin**donga	wall
ucango	**iin**gcango	door
usiba	**iin**tsiba	pen
usuku	**iin**tsuku	24-hour day
usana	**iin**tsana	baby
usapho	**iin**tsapho	family
uncedo	–	help
uxolo	–	peace
usizi	–	pity
ubisi	–	milk
udaka	–	mud
uthuli	–	dust

ucango

usana

- Nouns of Class 11 take the prefix **ulu-** or **u-** depending on whether the stem has one or more syllables.

- The plural, where appropriate, is in Class 10
  Notice the influence of **n**.
  - An **h** is always dropped if there is an **n** in the previous syllable of a word
    uluthi   →   izin**ti**   sticks
  - n becomes **m** before p, b, f and v: izi**m**vo   opinions
  - n + c   →   n**g**c   iin**g**cango   doors
  - n + s   →   n**ts**   iin**ts**ana   babies

- **ul**wandle   **ii**lwandle   11 & 10   sea
  ulwimi   **ii**lwimi   11 & 10   language
  ulwimi   **ama**lwimi   11 & 6   tongue

- Class 1a and Class 11 nouns both have the prefix **u-**. If unsure, the noun will generally be in Class 11. (Class 1a consists of people's names, kinship terms and a few special nouns).

Class 14

No plural
Prefix: ubu-

ubusuku	night
ubusika	winter
ubuso	face
ubusi	honey
ubushushu	heat
ubudala	age
ububele	kindness
ubuntu	humanity
ubuntwana	childhood
ubuzali	parenthood
ubuhlobo	friendship
ubomi	life
uboya	wool, hair (of animals or on the body)
*****ubu**hlanti	cattle-kraal
*****utyw**ala	beer, strong drink

ubuso

ubusi

N O T E

- Most nouns in Class 14 are abstract nouns.
- *These two nouns do have plurals.

Class 15

No plural
Prefix: uku-

ukutya

ukutya	food, eating
ukufa	death, dying
ukufika	arrival, arriving
ukufunda	learning
ukubhala	writing

ukufa

NOTE

- All verbs in their basic form, that is, the infinitive (**uku-** + verb stem), fall into Class 15 and can thus also be treated as nouns.
  Ndithanda **ukufunda**   I like **learning** (or books)

- If the verb stem begins with a vowel, the prefix **uku-** changes as follows:
before **a**	**ukw**azi	to know/knowing
before **e**	**ukw**enza	to make or do/making or doing
before **o**	**uk**oyika	to fear/fearing

- **Ukw**indla (autumn) is an exception as it cannot be a verb.

Umsebenzi 1

Complete the following table (Noun Classes 11, 14 & 15)

	Class	Singular	Plural	Meaning
1		**u**donga		
2		**ubu**ntu	–	
3		**uku**thetha	–	
4		**ulu**vo		
5		**u**xolo	–	
6		**ubu**sika	–	
7		**u**sapho		
8		**uku**fa	–	
9		**ub**omi	–	
10		**u**cango		

SIGNIFICANT WORDS AND WHAT THEY MEAN

- **Ubuntu** translates as humanity, or *menslikheid* in Afrikaans, but it means far more than this.

  Buntu Mfenyana, a Johannesburg sociolinguist, says that to understand the full meaning of the word **ubuntu** one must first separate the prefix **ubu-** from the root **-ntu**.

  Ntu is an ancestor who got human society going. He gave us our way of life as human beings. It is a communal way of life which says that society must be run for the sake of all. This requires cooperation, sharing and charity. There should be no widows or orphans left alone – they all belong to someone. If a man does not have a cow, then give him a cow to milk. There should be no *ohlelelekileyo*, or deprived person. *Ubu* refers to the abstract. So *ubuntu* is the quality of being human. It is the quality, or the behaviour, of *ntu* society, that is, sharing, charitableness, cooperation. It is this quality which distinguishes a human creature from an animal or a spirit. When you do something that is not humane then you are being like an animal.

  The Mind of South Africa
  by Allister Sparks

- **Ubuhlanti** (Cattle-kraal)

  The Xhosa treasures his cattle, which play an important role in his life. His wealth is assessed according to the number of cattle he owns. The **ubuhlanti** is a place of great importance, not only because of its association with cattle but because the spirits of the ancestors linger in the kraal. It is usually made of thorn and other branches, like the **isibaya** (sheep fold). However, depending on the locality, it may be made of stone or brick. Married women are very rarely allowed into the **ubuhlanti**.

  The men hold their meetings at the **inkundla**, which is a clear space of ground between the **umzi** (or huts) and the **ubuhlanti**. Religious ceremonies such as marriages also take place at the **inkundla**.

Verb links for Classes 11, 14 & 15

Study the following examples

Usana **lu**yakhala	The baby (it) is crying
Ubusika **bu**yaqala	Winter (it) is starting
Ukutya **ku**yabanda	The food (it) is cold

Once again it is clear that the verb link is derived from the prefix of the noun.

Class 11	**ulu-** or **u-**	→	**lu-**
Class 14	**ubu-**	→	**bu-**
Class 15	**uku-**	→	**ku-**

Umsebenzi 2

Fill in the correct verb link and translate

1. Ubisi ....dulu
2. Utywala ....dulu
3. Ukutya ....dulu
4. Ubusika ....**ya**fika
5. Usana ....fana nonina
6. ....njani?
7. ....lungile
8. ....mnandi
9. ....shushu
10. ....**ya**banda

NOTE

- The **-ya-** is used with **verbs** (when final). It is not used with other parts of speech.
- Notice the impersonal use of the Class 15 verb link **ku- (it is)** in numbers 6 – 10.

The 15 Noun Classes

Class	Noun	Prefix	Verb Link
1	**um**ntu	um-	u-
2	**aba**ntu	aba-	ba-
1a	**u**tata	u-	u-
2a	**oo**tata	oo-	ba-
3	**um**thi	um-	u-
4	**imi**thi	imi-	i-
5	**ili**fu	ili-	} li-
	ixesha	i-	
6	**ama**fu	ama-	a-
7	**isi**fundo	isi-	si-
8	**izi**fundo	izi	zi-
9	**i**bhasi	i-	} i-
	intaba	in-	
	inja	in-	
	impuku	im-	
10	**ii**bhasi	ii-	} zi-
	iintaba	iin-	
	izinja	izin-	
	iimpuku	iim-	
11	**ulu**vo	ulu-	} lu-
	udonga	u-	
(10)	**izim**vo	izim-	} zi-
	iindonga	iin-	
14	**ubu**suku	ubu-	bu-
15	**uku**tya	uku-	ku-

NOTE

Strong Classes:	Verb link	=	**consonant + vowel**
Weak Classes:	Verb link	=	**vowel only** (shaded)

Verb Links with Vowel Verb Stems

Most verb stems begin with a consonant. For example: -**h**amba, -**t**hetha, -**z**a
There are some, however, which begin with a vowel and are thus called
vowel verb stems. These stems begin with the vowels **a, e** or **o**.

-**a**zi	know
-**e**nza	make, do
-**o**yika	fear, be afraid of

- The infinitive

ukwazi	to know
ukwenza	to make, do
ukoyika	to fear
Before **a** and **e**:	**u** becomes **w**
Before **o**:	**u** falls away

- -**ya**- becomes -**y**-

Ndi**y**azi	I know
Ndi**y**oyika	I am afraid

- When there is no -ya-, the **verb link changes** as follows
  i) Strong verb links: most use the consonant only.
     Abafundi **b**azi yonke into (The students know everything)
  ii) Weak verb links:

u	→	w	Umfundi **w**azi yonke into
i	→	y	Intombi **y**azi yonke into
a	→	–	Amadoda azi yonke into

2. Verb Links with other Parts of Speech (non-verbs)

Study the following examples

Anjani amavili?	How are (they) the wheels?
Zinjani iifestile?	How are (they) the windows?
Ipetroli **i**dulu	Petrol (it) is expensive
Iifestile **zi**mdaka	The windows (they) are dirty

NOTE

- When the verb link is prefixed to these words, it brings along with it the appropriate verb, **is** or **are**.
- This word can stand before or after the noun to which it is linked.
  Ipetroli **idulu** or **Idulu** ipetroli
- There is no -ya- because the words are not verbs.

Some words which prefix the verb link

- **Question words**

-njani?	how?
-phi?	where?

  Examples

Unjani uThemba?	How is Themba?
Baphi abantwana?	Where are the children?

- **Relative stems**

-shushu	hot
-mnandi	nice, sweet, pleasant
-mdaka	dirty, brown
-dulu	expensive
-tshiphu	cheap
-nzima	heavy; difficult
-lula	light; easy
-lusizi	sad
-manzi	wet
-buhlungu	painful, sore

Imibala/Amabala	The colours
-mnyama	black
-mhlophe	white
-bomvu	red
-luhlaza	green
-blowu	blue
-lubhelu	yellow
-ntsundu	brown
-ngwevu	grey

NOTE

The word for **colour** can be

umbala	**imi**bala	3 + 4
ibala	**ama**bala	5 + 6

Examples

Amanzi **a**shushu	The water is hot
IsiXhosa **si**nzima!	Xhosa is difficult!
Imoto **i**mhlophe	The car is white
Unyawo **lu**buhlungu	The foot is sore
Izihlangu **zi**bomvu	The shoes are red

amanzi ashushu

NOTE

- Imoto **i**mhlophe   The car **is** white (**not:** The white car)

- In English we call these words adjectives. In Xhosa they are called relative stems. Relatives prefix the verb link, when used as above. (There are only 18 adjective stems in Xhosa. They prefix their own set of links and will not be dealt with.)

- **Words indicating place**

phandle	outside
phakathi	inside
phantsi	down, below
phezu**lu**	up, above
phambi**li**	in front
emva	behind, at the back
ecaleni	at/on the side, next to

Examples

Abazali **ba**phakathi	The parents are inside
Ilanga **li**phezulu	The sun is high up
Imoto **i**phambili	The car is in front
Iimpahla **zi**semva*	The goods are in/at the back
Umthi **u**secaleni*	The tree is on the side

NOTE

- *The **s** is a buffer, used before **e**, to separate the two vowels.

- These words can all prefix **nga-**.
  This seems to make the meaning general, rather than specific.
  ngaphambili   'round about' the front
  ngasemva   'round about' the back

- When followed by a noun, these words take **kwa-**, **kwe-** or **ko-** depending on whether the noun begins with **a, i** or **u**.

ecaleni	**kwa**manzi	at the side of the water
ngaphandle	**ko**Mzantsi Afrika	outside South Africa
*phezu	**kwe**tafile	on top of the table
*phambi	**ko**cango	in front of the door

*These two words drop the last syllable (**-lu, -li**) when followed by a noun.

- ***Other words indicating place***

apha	here
apho	there
phaya	over there, yonder
khona	be present/there

Examples

Amanzi a̱lapha	The water is here (in the kitchen)
Indlu i̱lapho	The house is there (next to those trees)
Baphaya	They are over there (at the river)
Sikhona	We are present (Also: We are fine)

(The **l** is a buffer used before **apha** and **apho**)

Learn the following

- **apha nalapho** — **here and there**
- Yiza **ngapha** — Come **in this direction**
- Jonga **phaya** — Look **over there**
- Utata **ukhona/ukho** — Father is **present/here**
- Bahlala **khona** — They live **there/in that place**

Nouns used to express place (locatives)

e**Kapa**	**in** Cape Town
e**khaya**	**at** home
e**tafil**eni	**on** the table
e**msebenz**ini	**at** work
e**sikol**weni	**at** school

Examples

ULizo **us**eKapa	Lizo is in Cape Town
Umakhulu **us**ekhaya	Grandmother is at home
Incwadi **is**etafileni	The book is on the table
Utata **us**emsebenzini	Father is at work
Abantwana **bas**esikolweni	The children are at school

NOTE

When a verb link is used with a word expressing **place** which starts with **e-**, an **-s-** is inserted between the two vowels as a **buffer**. It is called the pre-locative **s**.

Revise all the verb links thoroughly (page 105), as well as the vocabulary for the chapter (page 117), and then complete the following five exercises.

Umsebenzi 3

Fill in the correct verb links (Classes 11, 14 & 15) and translate
1. Ukutya ....dulu
2. Ubisi ....shushu
3. Ucango ....bomvu
4. Ukuthetha ....nzima
5. Ubusuku ....mnyama
6. Ulwandle ....blowu
7. Ukubhala ....lula
8. Ubomi ....nzima
9. Uzwane ....buhlungu
10. Ubushushu ....mnandi

Umsebenzi 4

Answer the following questions as shown in the example

Iphi moto?	(egaraji)	**is**egaraji	It is in the garage
1. Uphi uThandi?	(endlwini)		
2. Siphi isitshixo?	(emotweni)		
3. Baphi ootata?	(emsebenzini)		
4. Iphi inkosikazi?	(esibhedlele)		
5. Uphi umama?	(ekhitshini)		
6. Liphi ikhaya?	(emaXhoseni)		
7. Iphi indoda?	(entolongweni)		
8. Luphi ubisi?	(efrijini)		
9. Buphi ubusi?	(etafileni)		
10. Kuphi ukutya?	(ekhabhathini)		

Umsebenzi 5

*Use **njani** (how) with each of the following nouns as shown in the example*
e.g. uLindi   Unjani uLindi?   How is Lindi?

1. umama
2. ootata
3. inkosikazi yakho
4. umyeni wakho
5. abantwana

6. umsebenzi
7. isikolo
8. ibala
9. impilo
10. ubomi

Umsebenzi 6

Complete the following using the correct verb link and translate

1. UMary (phandle)
2. Izinja (phakathi)
3. Abantu (phambili)
4. Igadi (emva) kwendlu
5. Umthi (ecaleni) kwendlu
6. Iimpahla (apha)
7. Isibane (phezulu)
8. Abamelwane (khona)
9. Amanzi (apho)
10. Isikolo (phaya)

Umsebenzi 7

*Complete the following using **kwa-, kwe-,** or **ko-** and translate*

1. phantsi + umthi
2. phezu + ikhabhathi
3. phambi + indlu
4. emva + ucango
5. ecaleni + umlambo
6. *phakathi + amaXhosa
7. *phambi + umsebenzi
8. *emva + imini
9. *phambi + ukuhamba
10. *emva + ukutya

Abantwana badlala phantsi komthi

NOTE

*The following words have two meanings:

phakathi inside or **between/among**
phambi in front or **before** (time)
emva behind or **after** (time)

The verb link ku- (it is) used impersonally

ku- with verbs (relating to the weather)

Kuyabanda	**It is** cold
Kuyavuthuza	**It is** blowing
Kuyana/**Ku**yanetha	**It is** raining
Kuyatshiza	**It is** drizzling
Kuyaduduma	**It is** thundering
Kuyatshisa	**It is** very hot (*lit*: burning)
Kupholile	**It is** cool

Kuyaduduma

Ku- with non-verbs

Kunjani?	How **is it**?
Kushushu	**It is** hot
Kumnandi	**It is** nice
Kubuhlungu	**It is** painful
Kunzima	**It is** difficult
Kulula	**It is** easy
Kuleythi	**It is** late
Kunjalo/**Ku**nje	**It is** like that/**It is** like this
Kuhle	**It is** beautiful/**It is** alright
Kubi	**It is** ugly/bad
Kukho.....	**It is** present ... (there is/are....)

NOTE

- -banda   be cold to the touch (things)
  -godola   be/feel cold (people and animals)
  ingqele   a/the cold
  Examples
  Kuyabanda namhlanje   It is cold today
  Ndiyagodola   I am cold
  Ndi**ne**ngqele   I **have** a cold
- Kushushu namhlanje   It is hot today
  Ndi**zi**va ndishushu   I am hot (*lit*: I feel **myself** I am hot)

Umsebenzi 8

'Linjani izulu?' (What is the weather like?)

Translate into Xhosa

1. It is beautiful
2. It is pleasant
3. It is cool
4. It is hot
5. It is very hot (burning)
6. It is raining
7. It is bad
8. It is cold
9. It is blowing
10. It is drizzling
11. It is thundering
12. It is raining

'Amaxesha onyaka' (Times of the year/seasons)

Fill in the blank spaces

1. Ekwindla, ... (it is cool)
2. Ebusika, ... (it is cold)
3. Entlakohlaza, ... (it blows)
4. Ehlotyeni, ... (it is hot)

INGOMA

Imvula	*The rain*
Imvula! Imvula!	The rain! The rain!
Chapha! Chapha! Chapha!	Drip! Drip! Drip!
Imanz' ilokhwe yam!	My dress is wet!
Gqum! Gqum! Gqum! Kuyaduduma	Roar! Roar! Roar! It is thundering
Imanz' ilokhwe yam!	My dress is wet!
Imanz' ilokhwe yam!	My dress is wet!

INCWADI/ILETA • A LETTER

15 Park Road
Rondebosch
7700
15 Julayi 2005

Nomhle othandekayo

Enkosi kakhulu ngeleta yakho. Ndiyabulela. Iindaba zakho zimnandi kodwa ndilusizi ukuva ukuba uyagula. Mhlawumbi ubhetele ngoku. Thina, apha eKapa, sisaphila sonke.

Uthi kushushu apho eThekwini. Awu! Iholide imnandi! Nidada elwandle? EKapa kusebusika ngoku, kaloku. Kuyabanda, kuyana, umoya uvuthuza gqitha! Sihlala ngaphakathi.

Ngoku ndifuna ukukuxelela iindaba zam. Ndifunda isiXhosa! Ndifunda ukuthetha nokubhala. Kumnandi kakhulu kodwa kunzima! Emini ndiyasebenza, ebusuku ndiyafunda. Ndiyakwazi ukuthetha kancinci. Ukubuya kwakho ungandincedisa?

Khawubhale kwakhona kamsinya! Sukubhala ngesiNgesi!

Ngombuliso omkhulu
Umhlobo wakho
Karen

NOTE

- **Nomhle o**thand**ekayo** — Dear Nomhle (lit: **who** is love*able*)
  Mhlobo wam **o**thand**ekayo** — My dear Friend

- **Ngo**mbuliso omkhulu — Lit: **With** a big greeting
  Ndiyabulisa kakhulu — Lit: I greet greatly

Isigama

-va	hear
mhlawumbi	perhaps
-bhetele	better
sonke	all of us
eThek**wini**	**in** Durban
kaloku	by the way (remember)
-dada	swim
gqitha	a lot
uku**ku**xelela	to tell **you**
ukubuya kwakho	on your return
u**nga**ndincedisa?	<u>can</u> you help **me**?
khawubhal**e**	**please** write
kamsinya	soon
-bhal**ela**	write **to**
qha	only

Umsebenzi 9

Phendula le mibuzo

1. UKaren uhlala phi?
2. Ubhal**ela** bani?
3. Yena, umhlobo wakhe, uphi?
4. Izulu linjani eThekwini?
5. EKapa izulu linjani?
6. UKaren uneendaba .... Zithini?
7. Ufunda emini nasebusuku?
8. Kulula ukuthetha isiXhosa?
9. Wena, ufunda isiXhosa?
10. Uyakwazi ukuthetha isiXhosa?

*Ngoku, zama ukubhala ileta **ngokwakho**.*
*Now, try to write a letter **by yourself**.*

The following idiomatic expressions contain a relative stem:
(Both literal and idiomatic meanings are given)

- Ushushu
  He is hot
  He is drunk

- Umfazi unzima
  The woman is heavy
  She is pregnant

- Amehlo abomvu
  The eyes are red
  They are strained

- Amehlo amnyama
  The eyes are black
  They are blinded with emotion/a glare

- Amazwi amdaka
  The words are dirty
  They are obscene

In addition (Ukongeza)

Imidlalo (Games/Sports)

Umsebenzi 10

Nika isiNgesi
Umdlalo
1. ibhola yeenyawo/isoka
2. umbhoxo/irabhi
3. iqakamba/ikrikethi
4. intenetya/itenesi
5. ihoki
6. igalufa
7. isikwashi
8. ukubaleka/iiathiletiki
9. ukuqubha/ukudada
10. umdlalo wamanqindi

Udlala iqakamba

Isigama

	-mbhoxo	oval
5	**i**qakamba	a round, hollow object
5	**i-/ama**nqindi	fists

5	ibala/amabala	field
	ebaleni/emabaleni	on the field/fields
9	impempe	whistle
1a	unompempe/usompempe	referee
11	ukhuphiswano	match, competition

Umsebenzi 11

Translate into Xhosa
1. Do you like to play golf?
2. Running is nice
3. Boys and girls play hockey
4. We watch rugby and soccer in the weekend
5. The boys play cricket on the fields at school
6. It is nice to swim **when** it is hot (**xa**)
7. One (a person) plays squash inside
8. We play tennis on Saturday
9. They are watching boxing on television
10. Where is the field? Where are the fields?

Isigama
Nouns
Class

11	uluthi	stick
	uluvo	opinion
	uluntu	community
	ulutsha	youth, young people
	unyawo	foot
	(unwele) iin-	hair
	uzwane	toe
	udonga	wall
	ucango	door
	usiba	pen, feather
	usuku	24-hour day
	usana	baby
	usapho	family
	uncedo	help
	uxolo	peace
	usizi	pity
	ubisi	milk
	udaka	mud
	uthuli	dust
	ulwimi	tongue, language
	ulwandle	sea

14	ubusuku	night
	ubusika	winter
	ubuso	face
	ubusi	honey
	ubuhlanti	cattle kraal
	ubushushu	heat
	ubudala	age
	ububele	kindness
	ubuntu	humanity
	ubuntwana	childhood
	ubuzali	parenthood
	ubuhlobo	friendship
	ubomi	life
	uboya	wool, hair (of animals or on the body)
	utywala	beer, alcohol
15	ukutya	food
	ukufa	death
	ukwindla	autumn
3/5	umbala/ibala	colour
9	ikhabhathi	cupboard
9	impilo	health
9	ingqele	a/the cold
5/9	izulu/imozulu	weather
9	ibhola	ball
5	ibala	an open space, clearing, playing field

Verbs

-qala	start, begin
-banda	be cold (things)
-godola	be cold (people, animals)
-na	(to) rain
-netha	(to) rain, get wet
-tshiza	(to) drizzle
-duduma	(to) thunder
-tshisa	(to) burn
-phola	become cool
-va	hear, feel, taste
-dada/-qubha	swim
-bhalela	write to
-ongeza	add
-buka/-bukela	watch (with admiration)

General

-shushu	hot
-mnandi	nice, pleasant
-mdaka	dirty, brown
-dulu	expensive
-tshiphu	cheap
-nzima	heavy, difficult
-lula	light, easy
-lusizi	sad
-manzi	wet
-buhlungu	painful, sore
-mnyama	black, dark
-mhlophe	white
-bomvu	red
-luhlaza	green
-blowu	blue
-lubhelu	yellow
-ntsundu	brown
-ngwevu	grey
phezulu	up/above
phambili	in front/before
emva	behind/after
ecaleni	at/on the side, next to
apha	here
apho	there
phaya	over there
khona	be here/present; there
-pholile	be cool
leythi	late
njalo	like that
nje	like this
-hle	beautiful
-bi	ugly/bad
mhlawumbi	perhaps
-bhetele	better
sonke	all of us
eThekwini	in Durban
awu!	gee!
kaloku	by the way (remember)
gqitha	a great deal, a lot
kamsinya	soon
qha	only
ngokwakho	by yourself
ukongeza	in addition
xa	when

} Adjective stems in Xhosa

For vocabulary on **Sports**, see pages 116 & 117.

The Negative • Object Pronouns

1. The Negative

Study the following examples

Andihambi   **I** am not going
*****Aku**hambi?   Aren't **you** (singular) going?
Asihambi   **We** are not going
Anihambi?   Aren't **you** (plural) going?
*****k** is a buffer between the two vowels.

To form the **Negative** of the present tense:	1st and 2nd persons (pos & neg)
<ul><li>Prefix **a-** to the pronoun/verb link</li><li>Change final -a of the verb to **-i**</li><li>Drop -ya-</li></ul> For example: **Andi**boni = I do not see	ndi- → **andi-** u- → **aku-** si- → **asi-** ni- → **ani-**

Umsebenzi 1

Phendula imibuzo

1. Uyahamba?   Hayi, ...
2. Uyaqonda?   Hayi, ...
3. Uyafunda?   Hayi, ...
4. Niyasebenza?   Hayi, ...
5. Niyagoduka?   Hayi, ...

NOTE

- If there is a **noun** following a negative verb, it loses its initial vowel.
  Andiphungi kofu   I do not drink coffee
- Class 10 nouns   **Andi**tyi **z**ilekese   I do not eat sweets
  (**Andi**tyi lekese   I am not eating a sweet)
  Class 11 nouns: **Andi**funi **l**ubisi   I do not want milk

Umsebenzi 2

Rewrite the following sentences in the negative and translate

1. Ndibona umntu
2. Sifuna iti
3. Ndithetha isiJamani

4. Ndifuna ubisi
5. Sitya inyama
6. Ndinxiba ijezi
7. Sithanda iinyoka
8. Siyaphuma ngokuhlwa
9. Uyaqonda
10. Niyamamela

INCOKO

UNomsa ufonela uThandi.   *Nomsa phones Thandi.*
***Ku**ngoMgqibelo kusasa. Ifoni iyakhala.*

UThandi:	Hullo!
UNomsa:	Hullo! Unjani namhlanje Thandi?
UThandi:	Hayi, **akukho nto**. Kunjani kuwe Nomsa?
UNomsa:	Hayi, ndiphilile. **Akusebenzi** namhlanje?
UThandi:	Hayi, **andisebenzi**.
UNomsa:	Ufuna ukukhwela ibhayisekile?
UThandi:	Hayi **andifuni**!
UNomsa:	**Akufuni**? Kutheni?
UThandi:	Ndiyanqena!
UNomsa:	Kunjani ukuya **ezivenkileni**?
UThandi:	Kulungile, kodwa **andinamali**!
UNomsa:	**Ayinanto**. Singabuka nje!
UThandi:	Kulungile.
UNomsa:	Masidibane ngo 10 esitishini.
UThandi:	Kulungile. Bhabhayi!
UNomsa:	Bhabhayi!

Isigama

Ku..........	**It is** (on) Saturday
a(ku)kho nto	There is nothing (bad) i.e. I'm fine!
andi**na**mali	I do not **have** money
ayi**na**nto	It **has** nothing (it doesn't matter)
masidibane	**Let** us meet

The Negative Verb Links for Classes 1 & 2 and 1a & 2a

Study the following examples

Umntu **aka**hambi	The person is not going
Umama **aka**sebenzi	Mother is not working
Abantu **aba**hambi	The people are not going
Oomama **aba**sebenzi	Mother and others are not working

The **Negative Verb Link** for

Classes 1 & 1a is **aka-**
Classes 2 & 2a is **aba-**

Since most **people** fall into these classes, the links are used a great deal.

Umsebenzi 3

Complete the following sentences in the negative

1. UMary uyasebenza kanti uJenny ....
2. Utata uyahamba kanti umama ....
3. Umntwana uyabaleka kanti umfazi ....
4. Abazali bayatya kanti abantwana ....
5. OoLizo bayaphangela kanti oobhuti ....

Umsebenzi 4

Refer back to the incoko 'UNomsa ufonela uThandi'
and answer the following questions

1. UThandi usebenza ngoMgqibelo?
2. UNomsa, yena, usebenza ngoMgqibelo?
3. UNomsa noThandi basebenza ngoMgqibelo?
4. UThandi ufuna ukukhwela ibhayisekile?
5. Kutheni?
6. Baya phi ke?
7. UThandi unemali?
8. Badibana eposini? Badibana phi ke?
9. Ngabani ixesha?
10. Wena, wenza ntoni ngesiqhelo ngoMgqibelo?

Umsebenzi 5

Answer the following questions in the negative
1. Wena, uyaphangela?
2. Nina, niyaqonda?
3. Umntwana uyagula?
4. Abantwana bayagula?
5. UZola uyanqena?
6. OoZola bayanqena?
7. Abafana bacela icuba?
8. Umfana ucela isigarethi?
9. Wena, uyatshaya?
10. Nina, niyatshaya?

NOTE

If the word following a negative verb is an **infinitive** (**uku**hamba), or a **locative** (**e**sikol**weni**), the initial vowel may or may not be dropped, depending on the emphasis. Generally, the initial vowel is retained.

Umsebenzi 6

Translate into Xhosa
1. I do not want bread
2. I do not want to go
3. I do not work in town
4. Father does not work in the weekend
5. The children are not going to school today
6. Themba does not like to work
7. The students do not like to study
8. People do not smoke a lot today i.e. these days
9. Thandi does not live at home, she lives in a flat
10. Lizo does not ask to go, he just goes

The Negative Verb Links for Classes 3 to 15

Class	Pos	Negative Verb Link	Class	Pos	Negative Verb Link
3	u-	*awu-	9	i-	*ayi-
4	i-	*ayi-	10	zi-	azi-
5	li-	ali-	11	lu-	alu-
6	a-	*aka	14	bu-	abu-
7	si-	asi-	15	ku-	aku-
8	zi-	azi			

*Weak classes

See examples for the above classes in **Umsebenzi 7.**

NOTE

In most cases, the letter **a** is placed before the **positive** verb link. Where there is no consonant (the weak classes), one must be introduced, as shown below.

- **u** is associated with **w**   u-   →   **awu-**
- **i** is associated with **y**   i-   →   **ayi-**
- Class 6   a-   →   **aka-**

Umsebenzi 7

Translate into English

1. Umoya **awu**vuthuzi namhlanje
2. Imithi **ayi**khuli ebusika
3. Ihashe **ali**baleki
4. Amadoda **aka**sebenzi namhlanje
5. Isitshixo **asi**ngeni
6. Intombazana **ayi**funi ukuhamba
7. Izinja **azi**lali ngaphakathi
8. Usana **alu**khali
9. Ubusika **abu**pheli
10. Ukutya **aku**tshi

Positive and Negative Verb Links

Person	Noun	Positive Verb Link	Negative Verb Link
1st		ndi-	andi-
		si-	asi-
2nd		u-	aku-
		ni-	ani-
3rd (Classes)			
1 & 1a	**um**ntu	u-	aka-
2 & 2a	**aba**ntu	ba-	aba-
3	**um**oya	u-	awu-
4	**imi**moya	i-	ayi-
5	ihashe	li-	ali-
6	**ama**hashe	a-	aka-
7	**isi**tshixo	si-	asi-
8	**izi**tshixo	zi-	azi-
9	**in**tombi	i-	ayi-
10	**ii**ntombi	zi-	azi-
11	**usa**na	lu-	alu-
14	**ubu**sika	bu-	abu-
15	**uku**tya	ku-	aku-

NOTE

Strong Classes: Positive link   =   **consonant + vowel**
Weak Classes: Positive link   =   **vowel only** (shaded)

Umsebenzi 8

Complete the following
1. The **negative verb link** for
   Classes 1, 1a and 6 is ....
   Class 3   is ....
   Classes 4 and 9   is ....
2. The above mentioned classes are called .... because their
   positive verb link consists of a .... only.
3. The remainder of the classes are called .... because their
   positive verb link contains a ....
4. In order to form the **negative verb link** of the strong classes, merely prefix
   .... to the positive verb link.
5. The negative **verb** in the present tense always ends in ....

• Negative verb links with <u>vowel verb stems</u>

Ndiyazi	→	**And**azi	I do not know
Ndenza iti	→	**And**enzi ti	I am not making tea
Ndiyoyika	→	**And**oyiki	I am not afraid

N O T E

- andi- → **and-**   with a vowel verb stem
- In most cases the negative verb link loses its second vowel before a vowel verb stem
- There is no -ya- in the negative!

Umsebenzi 9

Rewrite the following sentences in the negative and translate
1. Ndazi impendulo
2. UThandi wenza into namhlanje
3. OoMhlaba bakha indlu
4. Intombi yoyika ubumnyama
5. Abazali bazi yonke into

• The impersonal use of the verb link <u>ku- (it is)</u> in the negative (with verbs)

Kuyabanda	→	**Aku**bandi	It is not cold
Kuyavuthuza	→	**Aku**vuthuzi	It is not blowing
Kuyanetha	→	**Aku**nethi	It is not raining
Kuyana	→	**Aku**ni	It is not raining
Kuyatshiza	→	**Aku**tshizi	It is not drizzling
Kuyaduduma	→	**Aku**dudumi	It is not thundering

N O T E

The English meaning can also be 'it does not get cold, it does not blow', etc.

- ## The stem <u>kho-</u> (be present) in the negative

  Used impersonally

Akukho xesha	There is no time
Akukho mali	There is no money
Akukho bantu	There are no people
Akukho msebenzi	There is no work
Akukho nto	There is nothing/nothing wrong

  Used personally

Ixesha **ali**kho	There is no time
Imali **ayi**kho	There is no money
Abantu **aba**kho	There are no people
Umsebenzi **awu**kho	There is no work

  Also

UThemba **aka**kho	Themba is not present/here/there
Isitshixo **asi**kho	The key is not here
Abamelwane **aba**kho	The neighbours are not there

Umsebenzi 10

Phendula imibuzo

1. Kukho umoya? Hayi, ...
2. Kukho indlela? Hayi, ...
3. Kukho ifoni? Hayi, ...
4. Kukho umyalezo? Hayi, ...
5. Kukho ingxaki? Hayi, ...
6. Utata ukhona? Hayi, ...
7. Abantwana bakhona? Hayi, ...
8. Imoto ikhona? Hayi, ...
9. Amanzi akho? Hayi, ...
10. Izinja zikho? Hayi, ...

NOTE

Whereas in the positive one may use **khona** or **kho,** only **kho** is used in the negative.

- **The verb na- (have) in the negative**

  Study the following examples

Andi**na**mali	I do not **have** money
Asi**na**xesha	We do not **have** time
Umfazi aka**na**mntwana	The woman does not **have** a child
Abantu aba**na**msebenzi	The people do not **have** work
Indoda ayi**na**moto	The man does not **have** a car

NOTE

- **-na-** (have) remains unchanged in the negative. The reason for this is that the noun following a negative loses its initial vowel.
- Class 10 nouns: Andina**z**incwadi   I do not have book**s**
                  (Andinancwadi)   I do not have a book
  Class 11 nouns: Andina**l**usiba   I do not have a pen

Umsebenzi 11

Answer the following questions in the negative

1. U**ne**ntloko?
2. U**na**bantwana?
3. Ni**ne**ngxaki?
4. Ni**ne**zinja?
5. Umyeni u**no**msebenzi?
6. Indoda i**nee**nkomo?
7. Abantwana ba**ne**zinto zokudlala?
8. Amadoda a**ne**cuba?
9. Iintombi zi**ne**mali?
10. UNomsa u**ne**foni?

Umsebenzi 12

Translate

1. I do not understand
2. Themba is not lazy
3. The girl is not wearing a jersey
4. The people do not want to work
5. I do not know
6. The children are not afraid of dogs
7. It is not cold today
8. There is no milk in the fridge
9. Mother and father are not present/here
10. We do not have money

Exceptions
- Andiva   I do not hear/understand
  Andiva kakuhle   I do not hear/understand well
  The **-a** of this verb does **not** change to **-i** in the negative.
- Ak<u>e</u>va   He does not hear/understand/'listen'
  a always   →   **e** before **-va**
  Ndiy<u>e</u>va   I hear/understand

-SA- and -KA-

These elements appear immediately before the verb stem.

-SA-	Positive:	Ndi**sa**phila	I am **still** well
	Negative:	Andi**sa**phili	I am **no longer** well

Examples
- U**sa**funda isiXhosa?   Are you **still** studying Xhosa?
  Hayi, andi**sa**fundi siXhosa   No, I am **no longer** studying Xhosa
- ULizo u**sa**sebenza?   Is Lizo **still** working?
  Hayi, aka**sa**sebenzi   No, he is **no longer** working
  -ya- is never used with -sa!

-KA- Negative only: Andi**ka**gqibi   I have **not yet** finished

Examples
- Asi**ka**tyi   We have **not yet** eaten
- Utata aka**ka**fiki   Father has **not yet** arrived

N O T E

-ka- has the meaning **not yet,** and thus the Xhosa verb must be in the **present tense**, because the action has not yet taken place. However, the English translation appears to be in the past tense.

Umsebenzi 13

Translate into Xhosa
1. I am **no longer** working at Shell
2. I have **not yet** seen anything (a thing)/anyone (a person)
3. Themba has **not yet** finished
4. The sun has **not yet** come out
5. It is **no longer** raining

NOTE

The following idiomatic expressions contain a negative.
Both literal and idiomatic meanings are given.

- Aka**na**ntloko
  He has no head/mind
  He is foolish/unintelligent
- Aka**na**mlomo
  He has no mouth
  He is speechless
- Aka**na**ndlebe
  He has no ear
  He does not listen
- Aka**na**similo
  He has no character
  He has a bad character
- Aka**na**nto
  He has nothing
  He is poor/he does not count for much OR
  He is a fine/okay person
- Ak<u>e</u>**va**
  He does not hear/listen
  He is naughty
- Ayi**na**nto/Ayi**na**msebenzi
  It does not have a thing/use
  It doesn't matter
- Akukho nto
  There is nothing
  There is nothing bad/all is well
- Akukho ndlela
  There is no way
  There is no escape/it cannot be avoided
- Akukho mazwi
  There are no words
  There is nothing to say

INCOKO

Esibhedlele	At the Hospital

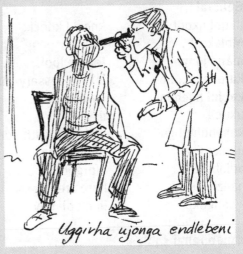

ISIBHEDLELE

Umguli: Nkqo! Nkqo! Nkqo!

Ugqirha: Ngena!

Umguli: Molo gqirha!

Ugqirha: Molo Mhlekazi! **Khawu**hlal**e** phantsi!

Umguli: Enkosi gqirha.

Ugqirha: Ngubani igama lakho?

Umguli: **Ndingu**Simon Mqondeki.

Ugqirha: Uhlala phi?

Umguli: Ndihlala eGugulethu.

Ugqirha: U**ne**minyaka emingaphi?

Umguli: Ndi**ne**-45.

Ugqirha: Kulungile ke Mnumzana
Mqondeki. U**na**ntoni?

Umguli: **Andazi** gqirha kodwa
andiva kakuhle.

Ugqirha: U**ne**ntloko?

Umguli: Hayi gqirha,
andinantloko.

Uqgirha ujonga endlebeni

Ugqirha: Uyakhohlela?

Umguli: Hayi gqirha, **andikhohleli.** Indlebe ibuhlungu nje.

Ugqirha: Heke, **ma**ndijong**e** endlebeni! **Musa ukoyika!**
Ugqirha ukhupha itotshi. Ujonga phakathi endlebeni.

Ugqirha: Kubomvu kakhulu ngaphakathi kodwa igazi **alikho.**
Kufuneka ugale**le** iyeza kabini ngemini. Kulungile?

Umguli: Kulungile gqirha.

Ugqirha: Thatha ipilisi kathathu ngemini.

Umguli: Ewe gqirha.

Ugqirha: Ukuba ku**se**buhlungu emva kweveki, **kufuneka u**buyel**e**
esibhedlele.

Umguli: Ewe gqirha, ndiyaqonda.

Ugqirha: Yima mnumzana! **Asikagqibi!** Ndi**sa**funa uku**ku**nika iyeza
neepilisi!

Umguli: Oo, uxolo gqirha. Ndilibele!

Ugqirha: **Ayinanto!** Nali iyeza! Nanzi iipilisi!

Umguli: Enkosi gqirha!

Ugqirha: Uyagoduka ngoku?

Umguli: Hayi gqirha, **andigoduki**, ndiya emsebenzini.

Ugqirha: **U**hamb**e** kakuhle mnumzana!

Umguli: **U**sal**e** kakuhle gqirha!

Isigama

Nouns

9	**i**totshi	torch
5	**i**gazi	blood
9	**i**pilisi	pill

Verbs

-khohlela	cough
-thatha	take
-ma	stop, stand
-libala	forget
-fumana	receive, get

General

nkqo! nkqo!	knock! knock!
Mhlekazi	Sir
mandijonge	**let** me look
kufuneka .....e	**it is** necessary/must (verb ends in -e)
kabini ngemini	**twice** a day
ukuba	if
ku**se**buhlungu	it is **still** (with non-verbs) sore
uku**ku**nika	to give **you**
ndilibele	I forgot
nanzi	here are (Class 10 nouns)
kwangoko	immediately

Umsebenzi 14

1. Uphi uMnumzana Simon Mqondeki?
2. Uthetha nabani?
3. Unentloko?
4. Uyakhohlela?
5. Unantoni?
6. Kukho igazi endlebeni?
7. Umguli ufumana ntoni kugqirha?
8. Ugoduka kwangoko?
9. Nika isiXhosa: It is **still** painful
10. Wena, unendlebe?

TRADITIONAL HEALERS AND RELIGIOUS BELIEFS

Despite the impact of Western medicine and the general use of it by Xhosa people, the influence of the **igqirha** (diviner or traditional healer) is still strong today, both in the rural and city areas. The **amagqirha** specialise in finding the cause and nature of misfortune and treating it. They work through the ancestors and by questioning their patients closely.

Another specialist in Xhosa society is the **ixhwele** (herbalist), who does not deal with the supernatural but has a good knowledge of healing herbs.

The traditional religious belief of the Xhosa is in the **iminyanya** (ancestral spirits). They communicate with these beings asking them to provide for their needs and to protect them. The Supreme Being, **uQamata**, is not approached directly, but rather through the ancestral spirits. Today, many Xhosas combine Traditional and Christian (where God is **uThixo**) beliefs .

INGOMA

Nkqo! Nkqo! Nkqo! Nkqo!	Knock! Knock! Knock! Knock!
Vulani emnyango	Open (at) the doorway
Ze singene	That we may enter
Thina bes'kolo	We of the school

INGOMA • THE CLICK SONG

Igqirha lendlela nguqongqothwane
Ebeqabel' egqith' apha, uqongqothwane!

The traditional healer of the road is the toktokkie*
He was just passing by here, the toktokkie
*The knocking beetle

NOTE

The **q** click and some of its variations are well illustrated in these songs.

2. Object Pronouns

Person	Singular	Plural
1st	me	us
2nd	you	you
3rd	him, her, it	them

Study the following examples

Uya**ndi**bona?	Do you see **me**?
Ewe, ndiya**ku**bona	Yes, I see **you** (singular)
Niya**si**bona?	Do you see **us**?
Ewe, siya**ni**bona	Yes, we see **you** (plural)
Ndiya**m**bona (umfundi)	I see **him/her**
Ndiya**ba**bona (abafundi)	I see **them**
Ndiya**yi**bona (imoto)	I see **it**
Ndiya**zi**bona (iimoto)	I see **them**

NOTE

- The object pronoun takes the place of the object in a sentence.
  It cannot stand on its own as in English, and is in fact **not** a pronoun in Xhosa.
- It comes **immediately** before the verb stem.
- The **-ya-** is retained when using an object pronoun.

Object Pronouns

Person		Object Pronoun		Example
1st (sg)	**-ndi-**	Uyandibiza?		Are you calling **me**?
(pl)	**-si-**	Uyasibiza?		Are you calling **us**?
2nd (sg)	**-ku-**	Ndingakunceda?		Can I help **you**?
(pl)	**-ni-**	Ndinganinceda?		Can I help **you**?
3rd				
Classes				
1 & 1a	**-m-**	Ndiyambona	(uLizo)	I see **him**
2 & 2a	**-ba-**	Ndiyababona	(ooLizo)	I see **them**
3	**-wu-**	Andiwuthandi	(umoya)	I do not like **it**
4	**-yi-**	Andiyithandi	(imipu)	I do not like **them**
5	**-li-**	Andilithandi	(igazi)	I do not like **it**
6	**-wa-**	Andiwathandi	(amafutha)	I do not like **it**
7	**-si-**	Ndiyasifuna	(isitshixo)	I want it
8	**-zi-**	Ndiyazifuna	(izitshixo)	I want them
9	**-yi-**	Ndiyayivula	(ifestile)	I open it
10	**-zi-**	Ndiyazivula	(iifestile)	I open them
11	**-lu-**	Ndiyaluthanda	(ubisi)	I like it (milk)
14	**-bu-**	Ndiyabuthanda	(ubusi)	I like it (honey)
15	**-ku-**	Ndiyakuthanda	(ukutya)	I like it (food)

Strong classes: Same as the verb link
Weak classes: • A consonant + verb link   (shaded)
       • **Classes 1 & 1a = m**   (shaded)

Umsebenzi 15

Complete the following

1. While the object pronouns **-ndi-**, **-si-** and **-ni-** all contain a .... and thus remain unchanged, **-u-** is preceded by ....
2. In strong classes, the object pronoun is the same as the ....
   i.e. .... + vowel
   In weak classes:
3. 1 & 1a: .... bears no resemblance to the ....
4. 3 & 6:   .... precedes the verb links .... and ....
5. 4 & 9:   .... precedes the verb link ....

Umsebenzi 16

Answer the questions as shown in the example and translate
Ubona **uLizo**?   Ewe, ndiyambona.

1. Ubona **uMandisa**?
2. Ubona **ooMandisa**?
3. Ufuna **ilekese**?
4. Ufuna **iilekese**?
5. Utya **inyama**?
6. Utya **amaqanda**?
7. Usela **ubisi**?
8. Uthetha **isiXhosa**?
9. Uya**ndi**thanda?
10. Uya**si**funa?

Umsebenzi 17

Complete as shown in the example

Thandi is reading **a book**   She is reading **it**
UThandi ufunda **incwadi**   Uya**yi**funda

1. I am helping **mother**   I am helping **her**
2. We help (our) **friends**   We help **them**
3. I am learning **Xhosa**   I am learning **it**
4. The woman washes **clothes**   She washes **them**
5. The man wants **work**   He wants **it**
6. The child drinks **milk**   He drinks **it**
7. The children drink **water**   They drink **it**
8. Mother drinks **tea**   She drinks **it**
9. Father buys a **newspaper**   He buys **it**
10. Nomsa likes **Themba**   She likes **him**

135

The object pronoun with

1. A noun

Ndiyafunda	I am reading
Ndifunda incwadi	I am reading **a** book
Ndiya**yi**funda	I am reading **it**
Ndiya**yi**funda incwadi	I am reading **the** book

When the object pronoun is used **together with the noun** (as in the last example) emphasis is being put on that noun. In this way, the English **the** can be expressed. Notice that **-ya- is retained**, even though a noun follows the verb.

2. A question word

U**si**funda phi isiXhosa?	Where do you learn Xhosa?
U**zi**thenga phi iimpahla zakho?	Where do you buy your goods/clothes?
U**li**sela nini iyeza?	When do you take the medicine?

-ya- is **never** used with a question word.
The question word comes immediately after the verb.

3. An infinitive

Ufuna uku**m**bona?	Do you want to see **him/her**?
Ndicela uku**yi**boleka (imoto)	I request to borrow **it**

The object pronoun comes immediately before the verb stem.

4. The negative

Andi**ba**boni	I do not see **them**
Andi**ba**boni **a**bantwana	I do not see **the** children

If a noun follows a negative verb, which contains an object pronoun, the initial vowel of that noun is retained.

5. Vowel verb stems

Ndiya**m**oyika (ugqirha)	I am afraid of **him**
Ndiya**y**oyika (inyoka)	I am afraid of **it**
Ndiya**b**oyika (abantu)	I am afraid of **them**

Only the consonant of the object pronoun is retained.

NOTE

- Ndiya**m**azi — I know **him/her**
  Ndiya**b**azi — I know **them**
- Andazi — I do not know
  Andi**y**azi (into) — I do not know **it** (anything)

- Ndiyavuya uku**kw**azi   I am pleased to know **you**
- Ndiya**kw**azi ukuthetha isiXhosa   I know how to/I can speak Xhosa
  Andi**kw**azi ukuthetha isiSuthu   I cannot speak Sotho

The object pronoun for **you** (singular) <u>and</u> for **Class 15** is **-kw-** before **-azi**.

6. Instructions
Positive

Ndixelel**e** iindaba zakho	Tell **me** your news
Ndinik**e** ithuba	Give **me** a chance
Ndincedis**e**	Help **me**
Mbiz**e** (uNomsa)	Call **her**
Bancedis**e** (abantwana)	Help **them**
Yikhulul**e** (ijezi)	Take **it** off
Zitheng**e** (iilekese)	Buy **them**

*When an object pronoun is used in a positive instruction, the verb ends in **-e**.*

Negative

Musa uku**ndi**xelela	Do not tell **me**
Musa uku**ndi**hleka	Do not laugh at **me**
Musa uku**ndi**khathaza	Do not worry **me**
Musa uku**m**biza (uNomsa)	Do not call **her**
Musa uku**ba**khathaza (abazali)	Do not worry **them**
Musa uku**yi**khulula (ijezi)	Do not take it **off**
Musa uku**zi**tya (iilekese)	Do not eat **them**

*In the negative, the verb must end in **-a**, because of the **uku-**.*

Umsebenzi 18

Translate into Xhosa
1. Can I help **you?** (singular)
2. Can I help **you?** (plural)
3. I am pleased to know **you** (singular)
4. Are you learning Xhosa? Yes, I am learning **it**
5. We are buying **the** house
6. I like to read **it** (the newspaper) in the morning
7. Where do you keep **it**? (the butter)
8. I do not like (**it**) the wind
9. The child is afraid of (**him**) the doctor
10. Do you know (**it**) how to drive a car?
11. Please give **me** your number
12. Do not close **it**! (the window)

The reflexive -zi-

- There is only one reflexive pronoun in Xhosa. It refers to all the forms of **self/selves**.
- It is treated like an object pronoun and thus always comes just before the verb stem.

Uya**zi**fundisa?	Are you teaching **yourself**?
Ewe, ndiya**zi**fundisa	Yes, I am teaching **myself**

Umsebenzi 19

Translate

1. Ndiya**zi**bona esipilini
2. Uya**zi**sebenzela? (wena)
3. UMziwakhe uya**zi**sebenzela
4. Abantwana baya**zi**fihla
5. Musa uku**zi**khathaza!

Note

U**zi**va njani?	How do you feel? (within **yourself**)
Zifundise!	Teach **yourself**!
Zigcine kakuhle!	Look after **yourself**! (well)

INGOMA

Kha**ni**bone nang' umoya	Just **you** (plural) see here is the wind
Hu ... Hu ... Hu ...	Hu ... Hu ... Hu ...
Ungen' efestileni	It comes through the window
Ucim' isibane sam	It puts out my light
Uyaphuma	It goes out (of the window)
Ndiyasala	I remain
U**ndi**shiya emnyameni	It leaves **me** in the darkness
Zuhambe! Zuhambe!	Go! Go!
Hu ... Hu ... Hu ...	Hu ... Hu ... Hu ...

INCOKO

UNomhle noKaren bayasixoxa isiXhosa.
Nomhle and Karen are discussing Xhosa.

UNomhle:	Molo mhlobo wam! Uziva njani namhlanje?
UKaren:	Molo Nomhle! Hayi, ndiziva bhetele, enkosi! Kunjani kuwe?
UNomhle:	Hayi, kulungile, enkosi. Usafunda isiXhosa?
UKaren:	Ewe, ndiyasithanda kakhulu isiXhosa.
UNomhle:	UMolly, yena, usafunda naye?
UKaren:	Hayi, akasafundi yena. Akalifumani ixesha.
UNomhle:	Oo, ndilusizi. UMnumzana Mlambo uyanifundisa?
UKaren:	Ewe, uyasifundisa. Uyamazi?
UNomhle:	Ewe, ndiyamazi. Ngumhlobo katata kaloku.
UKaren:	Oo, ndiyakhumbula ngoku.
UNomhle:	Ndingayibona incwadi yakho?
UKaren:	Ewe, ngokuqinisekileyo. Nantsi! Yijonge!
UNomhle:	Awu! Nifunda ukusithetha, ukusifunda nokusibhala isiXhosa.
UKaren:	Ewe usifundisa kakuhle utitshala.
UNomhle:	Ndixelele Karen, umntu uyithenga phi le ncwadi?
UKaren:	Uyifumana eCNA.
UNomhle:	Yimalini?
UKaren:	Yi-R100 kuphela.
UNomhle:	Oo, itshiphu. Ndifuna ukuyithengela umhlobo wam, uBrian. Naye, uzama ukusifunda isiXhosa.
UKaren:	Hayi ke, kulungile. Ungayifumana khona.
UNomhle:	Ngubani ixesha?
UKaren:	Andilazi ixesha Nomhle. Andinawotshi.
UNomhle:	Noko, kufuneka ndihambe ngoku.
UKaren:	Kulungile. Uhambe kakuhle.
UNomhle:	Wena, usale kakuhle Karen. Mbulise uMnu. Mlambo!

Isigama

katata/kaKaren	of father/of Karen (Class 1a)
-khumbula	remember
kuphela	only
-thengela	buy for...
iwotshi	watch
noko	nevertheless, still

NOTE

- Sometimes the -ya- is dropped, even if the verb contains an object pronoun. This happens when the word following the verb is **not** a noun.

Ndi*zi*va **bhetele**	I feel (*myself*) **better**
U*si*fundisa **kakuhle**	He teaches *us* **well**
U*zi*fumana **eCNA**	You get *them* at **CNA**

- The object pronoun with **questions:**

U**si**funda phi isiXhosa?	Ndi**si**funda esikolweni
Uya**si**thanda?	Ewe, ndiya**si**thanda.

Umsebenzi 20

Phendula imibuzo

1. UKaren u**zi**va njani?
2. Uthanda uku**si**funda isiXhosa?
3. UMolly usafunda isiXhosa?
4. Kutheni?
5. UNomhle uya**m**azi utitshala kaKaren?
6. Ngubani igama lakhe?
7. UNomhle ucela ukubona ntoni?
8. Ufuna ukuthengela bani incwadi?
9. Umntu u**yi**thenga phi le ncwadi?
10. UKaren unewotshi? Wena, unewotshi?

Umsebenzi 21

Listen carefully to the passage about Nomhle and Karen before translating into English.

UNomhle noKaren baya**si**xoxa isiXhosa. UKaren uya**si**funda. UMolly, yena, akasafundi. Aka**li**fumani ixesha. UMnu. Mlambo uya**ba**fundisa. UNomhle uya**m**azi kuba ngumhlobo katata. Uya**m**khumbula. UKaren uthi uba**fundisa kakuhle. UNomhle ucela uku**yi**bona incwadi yakhe. Umntu u**yi**fumana eCNA. Yi-R100 kuphela. Itshiphu. UNomhle ufuna uku**yi**thengela umhlobo wakhe, uBrian. Naye uzama uku**si**funda isiXhosa. UKaren uthi aka**l**azi ixesha kuba akanawotshi. Noko, uNomhle uyahamba.
Uthi: '**M**bulise, uMnu. Mlambo!'

Isigama

Nouns

Class

7	**isi**Jamani	German
9	**in**yama	meat
9	**in**tlanzi	fish
7	**isi**tishi	station
5	**i**cuba	tobacco
9	**i**sigarethi	cigarette
9	**i**flethi	flat
5	**i**hashe	horse
9	**im**pendulo	answer
14	**ubu**mnyama	blackness, darkness
9	**in**to yokudlala	toy
7	**isi**milo	character
9	**i**totshi	torch
5	**i**gazi	blood
9	**i**pilisi	pill
5	**i**gqirha	diviner, traditional healer
5	**i**xhwele	herbalist
3	**um**nyango	doorway
7	**isi**pili	mirror
7	**isi**bane	light
9	**i**wotshi	watch

Verbs

-nqena	be lazy
-tshaya	smoke
-khula	grow
-phela	come to an end
-tsha	burn
-nkqonkqoza	knock
-khohlela	cough
-thatha	take
-ma	stop, stand
-libala	forget
-fumana	receive, get
-boleka	borrow, lend
-khathaza	worry, annoy
-gcina	keep, take care of

-qhuba	drive, press on with
-fihla	hide
-cima	put out, extinguish, switch off
-xoxa	discuss
-khumbula	remember
-theng**ela**	buy **for**

General

a(ku)kho nto	there is nothing (bad)/all is well
ayinanto	it doesn't matter
nje	just
kanti	whereas
ke	then, and so
nkqo! nkqo!	knock! knock!
mhlekazi!	sir!
kufuneka ...... e	**it is** necessary/must (verb ends in -e)
kabini ngemini	two **times**/**twice** a day
-se-	still (with non verbs)
uku**ku**nika	to give **you** (singular)
ndilibele	I forgot
nan**zi**	here are (Class 10 nouns)
kwangoko	immediately
nang**u**	here is (Class 3 nouns)
emnyam**eni**	**in** the darkness
katata	**of** father (Class 1a)
kuphela/qha	only
noko	nevertheless, still
igama la**khe**	**his** name (Class 5 noun)
incwadi ya**khe**	**her** book (Class 9 noun)

|||||||||||

Useful Constructions

1. It is/They are ..... with Nouns

1. **Nouns in Classes 1, 1a, 2, 2a, 3 & 6 take the prefix NG- to express It is/They are.**

Study the following examples

Ngumfazi	**It is** a woman
NguThandi	**It is** Thandi
Ngabafazi	**They are** women
NgooThandi	**It is** Thandi and others
Ngumoya	**It is** wind
Ngamadoda	**They are** men

Umsebenzi 1

Guqulela esiXhoseni

1. It is a child
2. It is father
3. They are children
4. It is father and others
5. It is a friend
6. They are friends
7. It is an example
8. They are boys
9. He is a Xhosa
10. They are Xhosas

2. **Nouns in Classes 4 & 9 take the prefix Y- to express It is/They are.**

Study the following examples

Yinja	**It is** a dog
Yikati	**It is** a cat
Yincwadi	**It is** a book
Yimvula	**It is** rain
Yimithi	**They are** trees
Yimibuzo	**They are** questions

Umsebenzi 2

Guqulela esiXhoseni

1. It is a car
2. It is a boy
3. It is a girl
4. They are examples
5. They are laws
6. It is a man
7. It is a lady
8. It is a danger
9. They are rivers
10. They are guns

3. **Nouns in the rest of the Classes (5, 7, 8, 10, 11, 14 & 15) prefix the CONSONANT found in their class prefix, to express It is/They are.**

Study the following examples

Lixesha	**It is** time
Sisipho	**It is** a gift
Zizipho	**They are** gifts
Ziincwadi	**They are** books
Luluvo	**It is** an opinion
Bubusika	**It is** winter
Kukutya	**It is** food

Umsebenzi 3

*Give the correct prefix (expressing **It is/They are**) and translate into English*

1. iyeza
2. usana
3. izihlangu
4. iintombi
5. isithuthuthu

6. ubusuku
7. ihashe
8. ukutya
9. izindlu
10. usapho

Summary

To express **It is/They are** with nouns

- Classes 1, 1a, 2, 2a, 3, 6   prefix **NG-**
- Classes 4, 9   prefix **Y-**
- The rest prefix the **consonant** of the class prefix.

Umsebenzi 4

*Give the correct prefix (expressing **It is/They are**) and translate into English*

1. umfundi
2. abafundi
3. inyaniso
4. ithuba
5. uNomsa
6. oomama
7. ubisi
8. umona
9. amafutha
10. isifo

NOTE

- **Ng**ubani?   Who **is it**?
  Ngoobani?   Who **are they**?
- **Y**intoni?   What **is it**?
  Zintoni?   What **are they**?

Umsebenzi 5

Answer the following questions using the noun in brackets
1. Ngubani?   (uZola)
2. Ngoobani?   (ooZola)
3. Yintoni?   (inja)
4. Zintoni?   (izinja)
5. Ngubani?   (umntwana)
6. Ngoobani?   (abantwana)
7. Yintoni?   (isipho)
8. Zintoni?   (izipho)
9. Yintoni?   (icici)
10. Zintoni?   (amacici)

NOTE

- Ngubani **lo**?   Who is **this**?   (person)
  Ngoobani **aba**?   Who are **these**?   (people)
- Yintoni **le**?   What is **this**?   (thing)
  Zintoni **ezi**?   What are **these**?   (things)

Lo and **aba** generally refer to **people**:   Classes 1 & 2 and 1a & 2a.
Le and **ezi** generally refer to **things/animals**: Classes 9 & 10.
An interesting use of this construction (**it is/they are** with **nouns**) is to complain about something.
Question: Kunjani?
Answer: Hayi, kulungile enkosi. **Ng**umsebenzi nje! (**It is** just the work!)

Umsebenzi 6

Guqulela esiXhoseni
1. It is just the weather!
2. It is just the rain!
3. It is just the wind!
4. It is just the heat!
5. It is just the cold!
6. It is just the work!
7. It is just the children!
8. It is just the winter!
9. It is just age!
10. It is just life!

Umsebenzi 7

*Complete using the correct prefix to express **is/are** and translate*

1. UThemba (indoda)
2. UNothemba (umfazi)
3. Inkwenkwe (uSipho)
4. Intombazana (uSiphokazi)
5. Abantwana (amakhwenkwe)
6. Imoto (iToyota)
7. Ulwimi (isiXhosa)
8. Umfana (ititshala)
9. Utata (unovenkile)
10. Ummelwane (ugqirha)

Summary

It is/they are .... with

- **Pronouns** (1st and 2nd persons)
- **Nouns** (3rd person)

1st Person		
(sg)	**Ndi**m	**It is** I/me
(pl)	**Si**thi	**It is** us
2nd Person		
(sg)	**Ng**uwe	**It is** you
(pl)	**Ni**ni	**It is** you
3rd Person		
Class		
1	**Ng**umhlobo	**It is** a friend
1a	**Ng**umama	**It is** mother
2	**Ng**abahlobo	**They** are friends
2a	**Ng**oomama	**It is** mother and others
3	**Ng**umthetho	**It is** a law
4	**Y**imithetho	**They** are laws
5	**L**iwele	**It is** a twin
6	**Ng**amawele	**They are** twins
7	**S**isibane	**It is** a light
8	**Z**izibane	**They are** lights
9	**Y**intombi	**It is** a girl
10	**Z**iintombi	**They are** girls
11	**L**uthuli	**It is** dust
14	**B**ububele	**It is** kindness
15	**K**ukuthetha	**It is** talking

- The final syllable of the first and second persons comes from the absolute pronoun.

  | 1st Person: | ndi**m** | (**m**na) | si**thi** | (**thi**na) |
  | 2nd Person: | ngu**we** | (**we**na) | ni**ni** | (**ni**na) |

- **U**ngubani? Who are **you**? **U**ngubani? Who is **he/she**?
  NdinguPeter I am Peter **U**ngumhlobo **He/she** is a friend

- Sometimes, the verb link is used in front, mostly for emphasis.
  UFana **ng**umhlobo Fana is a friend
  UFana **u**ngumhlobo Fana (he) is a friend

INCOKO

Ngumhlobo wam. **It is** my friend.
UNoxolo noFana batyelela uMandisa.

Ngumhlobo wam
ikeki
iilekese

	Nkqo! Nkqo! Nkqo! Nkqo!
UMandisa:	**Ng**ubani?
UNoxolo:	**Ndi**m, uNoxolo!
UMandisa:	Oo, **ng**uwe Noxolo! Ngenani!
UNoxolo:	Molo Mandisa!
UMandisa:	Molweni! **Ng**ubani lo?
UNoxolo:	**Ng**umhlobo wam.
UMandisa:	Molo bhuti! Ndiyavuya uku<u>k</u>wazi.
UFana:	Molo sisi! Nam, ndiyavuya uku<u>k</u>wazi. Ndi**ng**uFana.
UMandisa:	Mna ndi**ng**uMandisa.
	Bayangena
UNoxolo:	**Ng**oobani aba?
UMandisa:	**Ng**abamelwane. **Ng**ooTaliwe.
OoNoxolo:	Molweni! Siyavuya uku<u>n</u>azi!
OoTaliwe:	Molweni! Nathi siyavuya uku<u>n</u>azi!
UMandisa:	**Y**intoni le Noxolo? **U**ndipha ntoni?
UNoxolo:	**Y**ikeki. **S**isipho.
UMandisa:	Hayi, unobubele! Enkosi kakhulu. **Z**intoni ezi?
UNoxolo:	**Z**iilekese. Ndiyazi ukuba abantwana bathanda iilekese kakhulu!
UMandisa:	Nithini bantwana?
Abantwana:	Siyabulela! Enkosi kakhulu sisi!
UMandisa:	Heke! **L**ixesha leti! Masiphunge!

NB underlined letters = object pronoun

Isigama

-tyelela	visit
u**ndi**pha	you give **me**
u**no**bubele	you are kind (you **have** kindness)
Nith**ini**?	**What** do you (plural) say?
Lixesha leti!	**It is** tea time (time of tea)
Masiphunge!	**Let** us drink!

2. My (-m) and Your (-kho)

Study the following familiar examples

1. umhlobo **w**am my friend
2. abahlobo **b**am my friends
3. igama **l**am my name
4. ifani **y**am my surname
5. izinto **z**am my things

Umsebenzi 8

*Rewrite the above using -**kho** (your) and translate*

Summary

To form the **possessive link**, a **consonant** is needed with **-a-**
- Most strong classes use the consonant of the class prefix
  ba-, **l**a-, **s**a-, **z**a-   (Classes 2, 2a, 5, 7, 8, 10, 14)
- **Weak Classes:**

u	→	w	**w**a- (Classes 1, 1a, 3)
i	→	y	**y**a- (Classes 4, 9)
a	–	a	a- (Class 6)

- **Class 11**   **lw**a-
  Class 15   **kw**a

Umsebenzi 9

Fill in the correct possessive link with these 'body parts'

1. **um**zimba	...m		6. **ubu**so	...kho
2. **in**tloko	...m		7. **isi**fuba	...kho
3. **ili**so	...m		8. **imi**nwe	...ko
4. **ame**hlo	...m		9. **um**lenze	...kho
5. **iin**wele	...m		10. **u**nyawo	...kho

148

'Introduce' the following people as shown in the example and translate

Umama   **Ng**umama wam   **It is** my mother

1. umhlobo
2. abahlobo
3. umyeni
4. inkosikazi
5. umntwana
6. abantwana
7. unyana
8. intombi
9. amawele
10. abazukulwana

3. Here is/are ...

Study the following familiar examples

Nanku uThemba!   Here is Themba
Nali ikhadi!   Here is the card
Nasi isitshixo!   Here is the key
Nantsi imali!   Here is the money
Nanzi iincwadi!   Here are the books

Summary

Each noun class has its own word to express **here is/are**.

Weak classes		Strong classes	
1, 1a	nan**ku**	2, 2a	na**ba**
3	nang**u**	5	na**li**
4, 9	nan**tsi**	7, 8	na**si** na**zi**
6	nang**a**	10	nan**z**i
		11, 14, 15	na**lu** na**bu** na**ku**
final vowel = verb link		na + verb link (for Class 10, insert <u>n</u>)	

Complete as shown in the example
e.g. **U**phi utata **w**am?   Nan**ku**!

1. ......phi imali ......am?   ....
2. ......phi iisigarethi ......am?   ....
3. ......phi isitshixo ......am?   ....
4. ......phi izitshixo ......am?   ....
5. ......phi umntwana ......am?   ....
6. ......phi abantwana ......akho?   ....
7. ......phi ikhaya ......akho?   ....
8. ......phi usiba ......akho?   ....
9. ......phi umsebenzi ......akho?   ....
10. ......phi amatikiti ......akho?   ....

4. All/Every/the Whole -ONKE

Study and learn the following examples

Molweni **n**onke!	Hullo everyone!
Sisaphila **s**onke	We are all still well
Wonke umntu	Every person
Bonke abantu	All people (everybody)
Lonke ixesha	Every time/the whole time
Onke amaxesha	All times
Yonke into	Everything
Zonke izinto	All things
Yonke imini	The whole day
Yonke imihla	Everyday

Summary

A consonant must be prefixed to the stem **-onke**.
- **Strong** classes take the consonant of the class prefix.
  bonke abantu, **l**onke ixesha
- **Weak** classes: u → w **w**onke umntu
  i → y **y**onke into
  a → – onke amaxesha

Umsebenzi 12

Complete the following and translate

1. ....onke sonwabile
2. ....onke abantu bonwabile
3. ....onke into ilapha
4. Iimpahla ....onke zimdaka
5. Amadoda ....onke ayasebenza
6. Ndisebenza imini ....onke namhlanje
7. ....onke umntu uthanda ububele
8. UThami uphangela ....onke imihla
9. Izikolo ....onke zivala ngomso
10. Izinja zikhonkotha ubusuku ....onke

NOTE

- **-onke** can stand before or after the noun.
- konke = at all
  Anditshayi **konke**   I do not smoke **at all**

150

Summary

My/Your • Here is/are • All/Every

Classes	Verb link + phi?	Noun	Possessive	Here is/are	All/Every
1 & 1a	**U**phi	**um**hlobo	**w**am?	Nan**ku**	**w**onke
2 & 2a	**Ba**phi	**aba**hlobo	**b**am?	Na**ba**	**b**onke
3	**U**phi	**um**nqwazi	**w**am?	Nan**gu**	**w**onke
4	**I**phi	**imi**nqwazi	**y**am?	Nan**tsi**	**y**onke
5	**Li**phi	**i**cici	**l**am?	Na**li**	**l**onke
6	**A**phi	**ama**cici	*am?	Nan**ga**	*onke
7	**Si**phi	**isi**hlangu	**s**am?	Na**si**	**s**onke
8	**Zi**phi	**izi**hlangu	**z**am?	Na**zi**	**z**onke
9	**I**phi	**in**cwadi	**y**am?	Nan**tsi**	**y**onke
10	**Zi**phi	**ii**ncwadi	**z**am?	Nan**zi**	**z**onke
11	**Lu**phi	**u**siba	**lw**am?	Na**lu**	**l**onke
14	**Bu**phi	**ubu**si	**b**am?	Na**bu**	**b**onke
15	**Ku**phi	**uku**tya	**kw**am?	Na**ku**	**k**onke

NOTE

- All of **us**　　　　　**s**onke
  All of **you** (plural)　**n**onke
- The weak classes are shaded.

Listen carefully to the following passage before translating into English.

UThemba uthetha ngaye nangosapho lwakhe
Themba speaks about himself and about his family

Mna, ndi**ngu**Themba Majola. Ndi**ngu**novenkile. Nditshatile.
Sihlala eGugulethu, eKapa. Sinabantwana. Bathathu. **Ng**amakhwenkwe
nentombi. Basafunda esikolweni.
Abazali bam badala. Bona, bahlala eMonti.

UThemba ukhupha iifoto.

Nantsi inkosikazi **yam**, uNoluthando. Yena, uyititshalakazi.
Naba abantwana **bam**. Lo **ng**uVusumzi, lo **ng**uMandla, lo **ng**uNontombi.
Naba abazali **bam**. **Nanku** umama, **nanku** utata.
Nantsi ikati, **nanzi** izinja.

Thina sonke sonwabile apha ekhaya!

Isigama

nditshatile	I am married
-dala	old
sonwabile	**we** are happy

Ngoku, wena, zama ukubhala ngawe nangosapho lwakho.

UThemba Majola nosapho lwakhe – bonwabile ekhaya

5. 'Stative' Verbs

Stative verbs describe a state of action which is, in fact, taking place.

Present: Ndi**ya**lamba   I **am getting/becoming** hungry
Stative: Ndilamb**ile**   I **am** (in the state of being) hungry

Note the following stative verbs

-phila	→	-philile	be well (in health)
-lunga	→	-lungile	be good/fine
-phola	→	-pholile	be cool
-tyeba	→	-tyebile	be fat
-bhitya	→	-bhityile	be thin
-phela	→	-phelile	be finished (come to an end)
-lamba	→	-lambile	be hungry
-baluleka	→	-balulekile	be important
-tshata	→	-tshatile	be married
-coceka	→	-cocekile	be clean
-oma	→	-omile	be dry
-onwaba	→	-onwabile	be happy

Exceptions (in the endings)

-dinwa	→	-diniwe	be tired
-nxanwa	→	-nxaniwe	be thirsty
-hlutha	→	-hluthi	be 'full' (of food!)
*-hlala	→	-hleli	be seated
*-lala	→	-lele	be asleep

NOTE

- These verbs have two sides to them in the present tense.
  1. The present: Ku**ya**phola   It is **getting/becoming** cool
     The 'state' has not yet been reached
  2. The stative: Kuphol**ile**   It **is** cool
     The 'state' has been reached.

- * -Hlala and *-lala are different
  1. Ngesiqhelo si**hlala** apha   Usually we **sit** here
     Si**hleli** etafileni   We **are seated** at the table
  2. Ngesiqhelo abantu ba**lala** ebusuku   Usually people **sleep** at night
     Umntwana u**lele**   The child **is asleep**

Guqulela esiNgesini

1. Ndiphilile
2. Yonke into ilungile
3. Umoya upholile
4. Indoda ityebile kakhulu
5. Inkwenkwe ibhityile
6. Isonka siphelile
7. Nilambile?
8. Imfundo ibalulekile kakhulu
9. Utshatile?
10. Ihempe icocekile
11. Ivasi yomile
12. Sonke sonwabile
13. Usana ludiniwe
14. Inja inxaniwe
15. Ndihluthi!
16. Abantu bahleli engceni
17. Abantwana balele
18. UFana unyanisile
19. Kupholile emthunzini
20. Kubalulekile ukusazi isiXhosa

Umsebenzi 15

Guqulela esiXhoseni

1. I am getting fat
2. You are getting thin
3. The sugar is coming to an end
4. The people are getting hungry
5. Are you becoming tired?
6. I am fat
7. You are thin
8. The sugar is finished
9. The people are hungry
10. Are you tired?

NB

-phela	come to an end (be finished)
-gqiba	finish (doing something)
Ukutya kuphel**ile**	The food is finished **(stative)**
Ndigqib**ile**	I have finished **(past tense)**

N O T E

- -nqabile   be scarce   **Unqabile!**   (You are 'scarce')
  -ngxamile be in a hurry   **Ndingxamile!** (I am in a hurry)
  -xakekile   be busy   **Uxakekile?**   (Are you busy?)
  The above three stative verbs may appear to look or sound similar,
  but they are in fact very different. Practise using them.

- -nyanisa   speak the truth
  Unyanisile! You are right!
  Yinyaniso **It is** the truth

6. Noun Derivatives

Study the following example
Umfundi u**funda** isi**fundo**   The student studies the lesson
As seen above, nouns can be derived from verbs in Xhosa.
In some cases, several nouns from one verb stem.

NOTE

- **-funda**   **study, learn, read**
  - 1 & 2   **um**fundi   student
  - 1 & 2   **um**fundisi   teacher, minister (of religion)
  - 7 & 8   **isi**fundo   lesson
  - 9   **im**fundo   education, learning
- **-sebenza**   **work**
  - 1 & 2   **um**sebenzi   worker
  - 3 & 4   **um**sebenzi   work, job, exercise
- **-dlala**   **play**
  - 1 & 2   **um**dlali   player
  - 3 & 4   **um**dlalo   game
- **-thetha**   **talk, speak**
  - 3 & 4   **um**thetho   law
  - 7 & 8   **isi**thethi   speaker
  - 9 & 10 **in**tetho   speech
- **-thanda**   **like, love**
  - 7 & 8   **isi**thandwa   loved one, beloved, darling
  - 11   **u**thando   love

7. Verb Endings

Study the following examples
UThemba ufund**ela** uviwo   Themba is studying **for** an examination
Umfundisi ufund**isa** abantwana   The teacher teaches the children
Abafundi bayafundis**ana**   The students teach **one another**

NOTE

From the above examples it is clear that the final **-a** of the verb stem can be
extended to alter the meaning of a verb. More than one extension can occur
in the same verb.
-fund**isana**   teach one another (cause one another to learn)

Three verb endings

1. The verb ending -ELA   (for *or* to/towards)

- **for**

-funda	→	-fund**ela**	study **for** ...
-sebenza	→	-sebenz**ela**	work **for** ...
-linda	→	-lind**ela**	wait **for** ...
-thenga	→	-theng**ela**	buy **for** ...
-vula	→	-vul**ela**	open **for** ...

- **to/towards**

-buya	→	-buy**ela**	return **to** ...
-bhala	→	-bhal**ela**	write **to** ...
-fona	→	-fon**ela**	phone **(to)** ...
-baleka	→	-balek**ela**	run **towards** ...
-xela	→	-xel**ela**	tell **(to)** ...
-guqula	→	-guqul**ela**	translate **into** ...

Umsebenzi 16

Answer the following questions using one of the words given beneath

1. Ulindela ntoni apha?
2. Ubhalela bani?
3. Uthengela bani iimpahla?
4. Nibuyela nini eGoli?
5. Utata usebenzela bani?
6. Indoda ivulela bani ucango?
7. Uxelela bani xa kukho ingozi?
8. Umfana ufundela ntoni?
9. Ufonela bani?
10. Abantwana babalekela phi?

Amagama

inkosikazi	emanzini	ibhasi	uSpar	ubugqirha
abantwana	ngomso	amapolisa	uLizo	abazali

NOTE

- **Ndi**lindele!   Wait for **me**!
  Ndibhalele!   Write to **me**!
  Ndifonele!   Phone (to) **me**!

- **-ela + -ni** is another way of asking **why** (for what)
  Usebenz**elani?**   **Why** are you working?
  Ufund**elani?**   **Why** are you studying?

- -qhuba   drive, press on with
  -qhub**ela**   drive **for/to**

ukuqhub**ela** phambili   to drive forwards/to progress
Example: Uqhub**ela** phambili kamnandi ngesiXhosa sakho!
You are progressing nicely with your Xhosa!

2. The verb ending -ISA   (cause to do)
Note the following

-funda	(study)	→	-fund**isa**	teach
-sebenza	(work)	→	-sebenz**isa**	use
-bona	(see)	→	-bon**isa**	show
-tya	(eat)	→	-ty**isa**	feed
-thenga	(buy)	→	-theng**isa**	sell
-za	(come)	→	-z**isa**	bring
-phakama	(stand/get up)	→	-phakam**isa**	raise, lift
-tsha	(be on fire)	→	-tsh**isa**	burn
-bila	(boil)	→	-bil**isa**	make boil
-khula	(grow)	→	-khul**isa**	make grow, bring up

Umsebenzi 17

Guqulela esiNgesini
1. UThemba ufuna ukuthengisa imoto yakhe
2. Phakamisa isandla ukuba uyavuma!
3. Kunzima ukukhulisa abantwana
4. Ilanga liyatshisa namhlanje
5. Usebenzisa ipensile okanye usiba?
6. Ndibonise umsebenzi wakho!
7. Bilisa amanzi!
8. Sityisa iikati nenja ngokuhlwa
9. UMnu Mlambo ufundisa isiXhosa
10. Zisa iimpahla zakho!

Exceptions

-vu**k**a	→	-vu**s**a (wake someone)	Vusa umntwana!	Wake the child!
-khumbu**l**a	→	-khumbu**z**a (remind)	**Ndi**khumbu**ze**!	Remind **me**!

3. The verb ending -ANA   (one another/each other)

-bona	→	-bon**ana**	see **one another**
-thanda	→	-thand**ana**	love **one another**
-qonda	→	-qond**ana**	understand **one another**
-ncedisa	→	-ncedis**ana**	help **each another**
-bulisa	→	-bulis**ana**	greet **one another**

Umsebenzi 18

Guqulela esiNgesini
1. Ngesiqhelo sibonana ngeCawa ecaweni
2. Abasebenzi bayabulisana kusasa
3. UThemba noNomsa bayaqondana
4. Abantwana bam bayathandana
5. Kubalulekile ukuncedisana

Umsebenzi 19

*Give the correct form of the verb in brackets (**-ela, -isa, -ana**) and translate*
1. Ubhuti .... uMnu Taliwe   (-sebenza)
2. Abahlobo ....   (-ncedisa)
3. Utata .... umhambi indlela   (-bona)
4. Intombi nomfana ....   (-thanda)
5. Abantwana .... esikolweni ngomso (-buya)
6. Indoda .... bani?   (-linda)
7. Umama .... amanzi eketileni   (-bila)
8. UMeri .... abazali ileta   (-bhala)
9. UMnu Mbiza .... iimoto   (-thenga)
10. Umfazi .... abantwana izipho   (-thenga)

INCOKO

Isicelo somsebenzi   An application for work
Eofisini kaNkosk Zuma. Ufuna unobhala.

UZuma:	Molo nkosikazi!
UNdlovu:	Molo nkosikazi!
UZuma:	**Ndingu**Xoliswa Zuma. Wena ungubani?
UNdlovu:	Mna, **ndingu**Thami Ndlovu
UZuma:	Ndiyavuya ukukwazi
UNdlovu:	Nam, ndiyavuya ukukwazi
UZuma:	**Khawu**hlal**e** phantsi
	Bobabini bahlala phantsi
UZuma:	Kuqala, ndifuna ukubuza imibuzo **nga**we
UNdlovu:	Kulungile
UZuma:	Uhlala phi?

UNdlovu:	Ndihlala eKhayelitsha
UZuma:	Uyasebenza?
UNdlovu:	Hayi, andisebenzi
UZuma:	Utshatile?
UNdlovu:	Ewe, nditshatile
UZuma:	Unabantwana?
UNdlovu:	Ewe, abantwana bam bathathu
UZuma:	Umyeni wakho, yena, uyaphangela?
UNdlovu:	Hayi, akaphangeli. Uyagula
UZuma:	Nkosikazi, unereferensi?
UNdlovu:	Ewe, ndinayo. Nantsi!
UZuma:	Enkosi
	Uyayijonga ireferensi
UZuma:	Ilungile kakhulu. Uyakwazi ukusebenzisa ikhompyutha?
UNdlovu:	Ewe, ndiyakwazi
UZuma:	Hayi ke, kulungile. Sibhatala iR6000 **nge**nyanga
UNdlovu:	Ilungile
UZuma:	Uya**wu**funa lo msebenzi?
UNdlovu:	Ewe, ndiya**wu**funa
UZuma:	U**nga**qala nini?
UNdlovu:	Ndi**nga**qala ngomso
UZuma:	Kulungile ke. Fika **ngo**8 kusasa
UNdlovu:	Kulungile. **Sobonana** ngomso
UZuma:	**U**hamb**e** kakuhle!
UNdlovu:	**U**sal**e** kakuhle!

Eofisini kaNkosk Zuma

NOTE

• -cela	ask for, request
isicelo	a request
isicelo **so**msebenzi	an application for work
	Lit: a request **of** work
ukwenza isicelo somsebenzi	to apply for a job
• Eofisini **ka**Nkosk Zuma	In the office **of** Mrs Zuma
• **lo** msebenzi	**this** job

Positive/Negative answers

• Uyasebenza?	Ewe, ndiyasebenza
	Hayi, **andi**sebenz**i**
• Utshatile?	Ewe, nditshatile
	Hayi, **andi**tshat**anga**
• Unabantwana?	Ewe, ndinabantwana
	Hayi, **andina**bantwana
• Umyeni wakho uyaphangela?	Ewe, uyaphangela
	Hayi, **aka**phangel**i**
• Uyakwazi ukusebenzisa ikhompyutha?	Ewe, ndiyakwazi
	Hayi, **andi**kwaz**i**

NOTE

- The negative ending of stative verbs is **-anga**

anditshat**anga**	I am **not** married
andiphil**anga**	I am **not** well
andilamb**anga**	I am **not** hungry
• andi**ka**tshati	I am **not yet** married

Umsebenzi 20

Phendula imibuzo

1. UNkosk Zuma noNkosk Ndlovu badibana phi?
2. UNkosk Ndlovu wenza ntoni?
3. Yintoni umsebenzi wakhe?
4. Kuqala, uNkosk Zuma ufuna ukwenza ntoni?
5. UNkosk Ndlovu uyasebenza?
6. Unabantwana? Bangaphi?
7. Uyakwazi ukusebenzisa ikhompyutha?
8. OoNkosk Zuma babhatala malini ngenyanga?
9. UNkosk Ndlovu uya**wu**fumana umsebenzi?
10. Ungena **nga**bani ixesha kusasa?

160

Sesiyahamba			We are going already
Ixesha limkile	} x2		It is late
Siy' emakhaya			We are going home
Ixesha limkile			It is late

Jabulani	} x2			Rejoice
Siyatshata namhla		} x2		We are getting married today
Jabulani	} x2			Rejoice
Siyatshata				We are getting married

WEDDINGS

A wedding, **umtshato**, is considered a great occasion among African people. It is a time for feasting and rejoicing. From far and wide people come to join the celebrations, which often last for days. The groom is required to provide compensation to the father of the bride for the loss of the services of a daughter. This *ikhazi or dowry is paid in cattle, after negotiations between the two families, as to the number of cattle to be paid. Nowadays the **ikhazi** can be in the form of money.

*The verb is uku**lobola**.

Isigama

Nouns

3	**um**zekelo	example	9	**in**tetho	speech
5	**i**wele	twin	7	**isi**thandwa	loved one, darling
11	**u**thuli	dust	11	**u**thando	love
9	**i**keki	cake	11	**u**viwo	examination
1a	**u**nyana	son	14	**ubu**gqirha	(profession of) medicine
3	**um**hla	day, date	1	**um**hambi	traveller
9	**i**foto	photograph	7	**isi**celo	request, application
9	**im**fundo	education	1a	**u**nobhala	secretary
9	**i**vasi	washing	9	**i**referensi	reference
9	**in**gca	grass	9	**i**khompyutha	computer
3	**um**thunzi	shade	3	**um**tshato	wedding, marriage
1	**um**fundisi	minister, teacher	1	**um**dlali	player
7	**isi**thethi	speaker			

'Stative' Verbs

-phila	become well	-onwaba	become happy
-lunga	become right	-dinwa	become tired
-phola	become cool	-nxanwa	become thirsty
-tyeba	become fat	-hlutha	become 'full' (of food)
-bhitya	become thin	-hlala	sit, live
-phela	come to an end	-lala	sleep, lie down
-lamba	become hungry	-nqaba	become scarce
-baluleka	become important	-ngxama	make haste, hurry
-tshata	marry, get married	-xakeka	become busy
-coceka	become clean	-nyanisa	speak the truth
-oma	become dry		

Other Verbs

-guqula	translate	-phakamisa	raise, lift
-guqulela	translate into	-tshisa	cause to burn, set on fire
-tyelela	visit		
-linda	wait	-bilisa	make boil
-sebenzisa	use	-khula	grow
-bonisa	show	-khulisa	make grow, bring up
-tyisa	feed	-vusa	wake someone
-thengisa	sell	-khumbuza	remind
-zisa	bring	-vuma	agree
		-jabula	be joyful, rejoice

General

konke	at all
-dala	old (adjective)
unyanisile	**you** are right (*also:* **he/she**)
kubalulekile	**it is** important
sobon**ana**	we'll see **each other**/see you!
bobabini	both (Class 2 & 2a)
mali**ni**?	how much? (**what** money?)

Summary Table

Person	Noun	Verb Link Pos.	Verb Link Neg.	Object Pronoun	Absolute Pronoun	Am/is/are + Noun	Here is/are	Poss. Link	All/Every/Whole
1st		ndi-	andi-	-ndi-	mna				
		si-	asi-	-si-	thina				
2nd		u-	aku-	-ku-	wena				
		ni-	ani-	-ni-	nina				
3rd Class									
1	**um**ntu	u-	aka-	-m-	yena	ng-	nanku	wa-	wonke
2	**aba**ntu	ba-	aba-	-ba-	bona	ng-	naba	ba-	bonke
1a	u**tata**	u-	aka-	-m-	yena	ng-	nanku	wa-	wonke
2a	**oo**tata	ba-	aba-	-ba-	bona	ng-	naba	ba-	bonke
3	**um**thi	u-	awu-	-wu-	wona	ng-	nangu	wa-	wonke
4	**imi**thi	i-	ayi-	-yi-	yona	y-	nantsi	ya-	yonke
5	**ili**fu } **ixesha**	li-	ali-	-li-	lona	l-	nali	la-	lonke
6	**ama**fu	a-	aka-	-wa-	wona	ng-	nanga	*a-	*onke
7	**isi**pho	si-	asi-	-si-	sona	s-	nasi	sa-	sonke
8	**izi**pho	zi-	azi-	-zi-	zona	z-	nazi	za-	zonke
9	**i**bhasi **in**taba **in**ja **im**puku }	i-	ayi-	-yi-	yona	y-	nantsi	ya-	yonke
10	**ii**bhasi **iin**taba **izin**ja **iim**puku }	zi-	azi-	-zi-	zona	z-	nanzi	za-	zonke
11	**ulu**vo **u**donga }	lu-	alu-	-lu-	lona	l-	nalu	lwa-	lonke
14	**ubu**suku	bu-	abu-	-bu-	bona	b-	nabu	ba-	bonke
15	**uku**tya	ku-	aku-	-ku-	kona	k-	naku	kwa-	konke

Points of Interest

1. Names (Amagama)

5/6	**iga**ma	**ama**gama	name
9/10	**ifa**ni	**iifa**ni	surname
7/8	**isi**duko	**izi**duko	clan name

First names (Amagama)

Giving a child a name is a great event. The child may be named after someone (an ancestor or some other important person) or after any event that coincided with the birth. Very often the name reflects what the birth of that child means to the parents. Thus:

Themba is hope
Sipho is a gift
Thandiwe is a loved one
Nomvula was born on a rainy day

Interesting points about Xhosa first names

1. These masculine/feminine names are **derived from the same stem**

Amakhwenkwe	Amantombazana		
Themba	Themb**eka**	**i**themba	hope
Sipho	Sipho**kazi**	**isi**pho	gift
Xola	Xol**iswa**	**u**xolo	peace
Thobile	Thob**eka**	**in**tobeko	humility
Lizo	Liz**eka**	**i**lizo	present

2. Some names have the **same shortened form** for both masc. and fem.

Lindile	**(Lindi)**	Lindiwe	-linda	wait
Thandile	**(Thandi)**	Thandiwe	-thanda	love
Lungile	**(Lungi)**	Lungiswa	-lunga	be good
Thamsanqa	**(Thami)**	Nomathamsanqa	ithamsanqa	luck

3. Some names have **several variations**

Vuyo, Vuyani, Vuyile (masculine)
Vuyiswa, Vuyelwa, Nomvuyo (feminine) } -vuya be glad
Xola, Xolani, Xolile, Mxolisi (masculine)
Thandiwe, Thandeka, Thandiswa, Noluthando (feminine)

4. Feminine names often prefix No-

Noxolo	**u**xolo	peace
Nosipho	**isi**pho	gift
Nontombi	**in**tombi	girl
Nokhaya	**i**khaya	home
Nomsa	**um**sa	love of a mother
Nomhle	**ubu**hle	beauty
Nombulelo	**um**bulelo	thankfulness
Nomhlobo	**um**hlobo	friend
Nomathamsanqa	**ama**thamsanqa	blessings
Nomathemba	**ama**themba	hopes
Nomalizo	**ama**lizo	alms (for the poor)

5. A **feminine ending** is -kazi

Sipho**kazi**	**isi**pho	gift
Vuyo**kazi**	**u**vuyo	joy
Mandla**kazi**	**ama**ndla	strength

6. An interesting aspect of Xhosa names is the **compounding of words**

Themba**lethu**	**Our** hope
Ntombekhaya	Girl of the home
Thandabantu	One who loves people
Mehlo**ma**ne	One who has **four** eyes (wears glasses)
Mandlenkosi	Strength of the chief
Jongilanga	One who can look at the sun without being hurt (One who can face any difficulty)

Surnames (Iifani)

Note the following surnames and the word from which each is derived

Mhlaba /Mhlabeni	**um**hlaba	earth, soil
Mlambo	**um**lambo	river
Nkosi	**in**kosi	chief
Ndlovu	**in**dlovu	elephant
Ludonga	**u**donga	wall
Ntaba/Ntabeni	**in**taba	mountain
Ngalo	**in**galo	arm
Ntamo	**in**tamo	neck
Madolo	**ama**dolo	knees
Mahlathi	**ama**hlathi	forests

Compare these surnames with the English
Butler, Butcher, Hill, Day, Knight
and Afrikaans
Appel, Swart, Kok, Blom, Visser

In all three languages the words from which some surnames are derived are easily recognisable, while those of others are not.

Clan names (Iziduko)

Clan names are of great importance in the Xhosa culture. They show the family into which someone was born, and can be traced back to the oldest male ancestor remembered.

The following are well known clan names:
Tshawe, Dlamini, Rhadebe, Madiba, Tshonyane, Tolo, Bhele.
Both men and women keep their clan names throughout their lives.
A woman usually prefixes **Ma-** to her clan name.
MaDlamini, **Ma**Radebe.

Using a clan name when addressing someone is a sign of familiarity or respect. The **royal clan** of the Xhosa is the **amaTshawe**.

NOTE

Ngubani **igama la**kho?   What is your **name**?
Ngubani **ifani ya**kho?   What is your **surname**?
Ngubani **isiduko sa**kho?   What is your **clan name**?

2. Place Names

Cities and towns (Izixeko needolophu)

In, at, to or **from:**

Alice	eDikeni
Bloemfontein	eMangaung (Sotho)
Butterworth	eGcuwa
Cape Town	eKapa
Durban	eThekwini (Zulu)
East London	eMonti
Grahamstown	eRhini
Idutywa	eDutywa
Johannesburg	eGoli/eRhawutini
Kimberley	eKhimbali
King William's Town	eQonce

Port Elizabeth	eBhayi
Pretoria/Tshwane	ePitoli/eTshwane
Pietermaritzburg	eMgungundlovu (Zulu)
Queenstown	kuKomani/kwaKomani
Mthatha	eMthatha

Provinces (Amaphondo)

Western Cape	INtshona Koloni
Eastern Cape	IMpuma Koloni
Northern Cape	UMntla Koloni
North West	UMntla Ntshona
Limpopo	ILimpopo
Free State	IFreyistata
Gauteng	IGauteng
Mpumalanga	IMpumalanga
KwaZulu-Natal	IKwaZulu-Natal

NOTE

- At the beginning of a sentence, the initial vowel is a capital letter but within the sentence it is a small letter eg.

  IMpuma Koloni inkulu   The Eastern Cape is big

  Inkulu iMpuma Koloni   It is big the Eastern Cape

- Notice that the **n** or **m** of the Class 9 prefix causes the **h** in the following syllable to fall away e.g.

  -**ph**uma   but   IMpumalanga

  -**kh**ulu   but   inkulu

- When expressing **Place** (in, to, from, etc.) the initial vowel becomes **e-**

  Kunetha kakhulu **e**Ntshona Koloni ebusika

  It rains a lot **in** the Western Cape in winter

  Except for:

  Bavela **Kwa**Zulu-Natal

  They come **from** KwaZulu-Natal

Isigama

7	**isi**xeko	city	*-phuma	come/go out	
9	**i**dolophu	town	*-tshona	disappear, go down, sink	
5	**i**phondo	province	**in**kulu	**it is** big (Class 9)	
9	**i**Koloni	The Cape			
3	**uM**ntla	North			

*With the provinces, these verbs refer to the rising and setting of the sun.

3. Nkosi Sikelel' iAfrika

Nkosi Sikelel' iAfrika is a hymn that was written in 1897 by Enoch Sontonga, who was born in Lovedale in the Eastern Cape and later moved to Johannesburg. It was first sung in public at the ordination of a Shangaan minister in 1899. Later, seven more verses were written by the poet Samuel Mqhayi.

Usually only the first verse and the chorus are sung in the **Xhosa/Zulu** version, followed by the **Sotho**, *Morena Boloka Setjhaba sa heso (Lord Save our Nation)*. There are variations in some of the words of the first verse, as is shown below. There are also variations in the order of the words, and the harmonisation.

Nkosi sikelel' iAfrika			*Lord bless Africa*
Maluphakamis' uphondo lwayo			*May her horn/ 'spirit' rise up*
Yiva nemithandazo yethu	} 2x	}	*Hear also our prayers*
Nkosi sikelela			*Lord bless*
Thina lusapho lwayo			*Us her family*

CHORUS

Yiza Moya	} x2		*Come Spirit*
Sikelela Nkosi sikelela			*Bless Lord bless*
Yiza Moya Oyingcwele		} 2x	*Come Holy Spirit*
Nkosi sikelela			*Lord bless*
Thina lusapho lwayo			*Us her family*

Variations

Maluphakam'/Maluphakanyisw'   *Yihla Moya /Woza Moya*
Yizwa imithandazo
Nkosi usisikelele

Professor Tim Couzens, a historian, writes that **Nkosi Sikelel' iAfrika** was composed as a hymn long before the founding of any of today's political parties. Furthermore, he says, it derived very definitely from a fusion of European and African culture. The hymn is, therefore, not an exclusive, but a common symbol. On the vexed question of language (no solution here can ever satisfy all groups) it goes some way towards reminding us a little about our past. The Xhosa, in which it was first written, contains the clicks which owe their origin to incorporation from the original Khoi languages.

Article from *Sunday Times* 13/10/93 by Professor Tim Couzens

4. Idioms (Izaci)

Many common Xhosa expressions have more than one meaning, the **literal** or obvious one, and a **figurative** or symbolic one. The latter enrich the language, making it more interesting. Often the arrangement of words in Xhosa cannot be translated literally or directly into English and remain meaningful. When one is aware of this aspect of the language, one starts to get a feel for the Xhosa of the mother-tongue speaker.

Study the following expressions which have more than one meaning

Utyebile	He is fat
	He is rich
Unesandla esishushu	He has a hot hand
	He is generous
Ukucela iindlebe	To ask for ears
	To ask for attention
Ukucela izandla	To ask for hands
	To ask for help
Ukucela amehlo	To ask for eyes
	To attract attention
Ukubeka inqawa	To put down the pipe
	To die
Ukugalela amanzi	To pour on water
	To criticise
Inyoka nesele	A snake and a frog
	Enemies
Kubi	It is ugly
	Things are bad
Ukuba shushu	To be hot
	To be drunk
Imfene yakho indala	Your 'baboon' is old
	You are late

Imfene yakho indala !

Isigama

	-beka	put (on/down)
9	inqawa	pipe
5	isele	frog
	-ba	be/become
9	imfene	baboon
	-dala	old

5. Useful Expressions

Imini emnandi	Happy Birthday
IKrismesi emnandi	Happy Christmas
INyibidyala emnandi	Happy New Year
IPasika emnandi	Happy Easter
Impelaveki emnandi	(Have a) nice weekend
Siyavuyisana na**we**/na**ni**	Congratulations (**singular**/**plural**)
	Lit: We rejoice with **you** (sg/pl)
Wamkelekile (sing)	Welcome
Namkelekile (pl)	Welcome
Ndiyabulela	I am grateful
Ndiyavuma/Andivumi	I agree/do not agree

Isigama

9	iKrismesi	Christmas
9	iNyibidyala	New Year/Nuwe Jaar
9	iPasika	Easter
9	impelaveki	weekend
	-vuyisana	make one another glad, rejoice
	-amkela	receive, accept, welcome
	-amkeleka	be acceptable, welcome
	-bulela	be grateful
	-vuma	agree

6. Tshotsholoza

The Xhosa people have a wonderful sense of rhythm. This is seen in their movement when singing, dancing and even walking. **Tshotsholoza** is a much loved song, which was often sung by groups such as road workers when working together. It is a reminder of how important it is to work as a team, and how a song can help to make life easier.

The words tell of a steam train coming over the mountains from the former Rhodesia (now Zimbabwe), bringing workers to the mines in South Africa. These days 'Zimbabwe' is often replaced by 'South Africa' in the song.

INGOMA • SONG

Tshotsholoza! Tshotsholoza! Uya kwezo ntaba
Stimela siphum' eZimbabwe } x2

Wen' uyabaleka! Wen' uyabaleka! Uya kwezo ntaba
Stimela siphum' eZimbabwe } x2

Isigama

7	**isi**timela	steam *train* (Zulu)	-tsholoza	sing joyfully
3	**um**culo	music	-cula	sing
5	**i**culo	song	-vuma	sing, agree
9	**in**goma	song	-danisa	dance (modern)
	kw**ezo** ntaba	along **those** mountains		

Tshotsholoza ... Tshotsholoza ...

Post Script

As you are now well aware, many words in Xhosa **look** and **sound** alike.

Nouns

- isel**a** — thief
  isel**e** — frog
- **u**xolo — peace
  ixolo — peel
- in**t**aba — mountain
  in**d**aba — matter
- ubus**uku** — night
  ubus**ika** — winter
- ubus**o** — face
  ubus**i** — honey
  ub**i**si — milk

General

- kub**a** — because
  ukub**a** — if, that
  ngoba? — why?
  kodwa — but

Verbs

- -**th**atha — take
  -**th**etha — talk
- -**dl**ala — play
  -**hl**ala — sit
- -**cu**la — sing
  -**ce**la — request
  -**se**la — drink
  -**su**la — wipe
- -ph**i**lile — be well
  -ph**e**lile — be finished/over
  -ph**o**lile — be cool

ubuso

ubisi

ubusi

An amusing anecdote to illustrate this point is that of the student who decided she wanted to put her newly acquired Xhosa into practice.

On her regular morning run, she passed a group of builders working on a house and she singled this out as a good place to start. Being on the move, she wouldn't be under any pressure to have to say too much!

She greeted the men, remembering to use the plural greeting **Molweni**, and to drop off the initial vowel of the noun following! Their response was not what she had anticipated. However, she tried it again the following day. Still to no avail. What was the problem, she wondered. "What did you actually **say**?", I enquired. "**Molweni mada̲da̲!**" she replied!

N O T E

amad**a**da — ducks
amad**o**da — men

172

ISIGAMA

Nouns

Class

Class			Class		
5	**i**gama	name	5	**i**phondo	province
9	**i**fani	surname	11	**u**phondo	horn
7	**isi**duko	clan name	3	**um**thandazo	prayer
5	**i**themba	hope	9	**in**qawa	pipe
9	**in**tobeko	humility	5	**i**sele	frog
5	**i**lizo	present	9	**im**fene	baboon
3	**um**sa	love of a mother	9	**i**Krismesi	Christmas
14	**ubu**hle	beauty	9	**i**Nyibidyala	New Year
3	**um**bulelo	thanks, thankfulness	9	**i**Pasika	Easter
			7	**isi**timela	steam ship
11	**u**vuyo	joy	5	**i**culo	song/hymn
3	**um**vuyo	joyfulness	3	**um**culo	music
9	**in**dlovu	elephant	5	**i**sela	thief
5	**i**hlathi	forest	5	**i**xolo	peel
7	**isi**xeko	city	5	**i**dada	duck

Verbs

-tshona	disappear, sink, go down
-sikelela	bless
-ba	be, become
-vuyisana	rejoice
-vuyisana na-	congratulate
-amkela	receive, welcome
-amkeleka	be acceptable, welcome
-bulela	be grateful
-tsholoza	sing joyfully, sing to dancers
-cula	sing
-vuma	agree, sing
-danisa	dance (modern)
-xhentsa	dance (traditional)

General

-ngcwele	holy
-dala	old (adjective)

For **Place Names** see pages 166 & 167.

Answers

Chapter One

Exercise 1

1. Hullo child
2. Hullo children
3. Hullo student
4. Hullo students
5. Hullo Nomsa and others
6. Hullo grandmother
7. Hullo grandfather
8. Hullo young man
9. Hullo young men
10. Hullo doctor

Exercise 2

1. Hullo father
2. Hullo mother and others
3. Hullo brother
4. Hullo sister
5. Hullo students
6. Hullo 'mister'/sir
7. Hullo 'lady'/mam
8. Hullo 'miss'
9. Hullo gentlemen
10. Hullo ladies

Exercise 3

1. Hamba kakuhle Themba
2. Hamba kakuhle nkosikazi
3. Hamba kakuhle mnumzana
4. Hamba**ni** kakuhle bantwana
5. Hamba**ni** kakuhle Nomsa
6. Sala kakuhle mama
7. Sala kakuhle bhuti
8. Sala**ni** kakuhle tata
9. Sala**ni** kakuhle makhosikazi
10. Sala**ni** kakuhle banumzana

Exercise 4

1. Molo mama
2. Molo tata
3. Molo mntwana
4. Mol**weni** bantwana
5. Molo nkosikazi
6. Mol**weni** makhosikazi
7. Molo mnumzana
8. Mol**weni** banumzana
9. Hamba kakuhle Nomsa
10. Sala**ni** kakuhle Themba

Chapter Two

Exercise 1

1. I am going
2. You are staying
3. I want **to go**
4. You want **to stay**
5. I like **Nomsa**
6. You are studying
7. I see
8. You speak **Afrikaans**
9. I need **a doctor**
10. I like **learning Xhosa**

Exercise 2

1. Ndi**ya**funda
2. Ndifunda isiXhosa
3. Ndithanda ukuthetha isiXhosa
4. U**ya**hamba
5. Ufuna ukuhamba

Exercise 3

1. Ndifuna ugqirha
2. Sifuna amanzi
3. Uthanda iti
4. Nithanda ikofu
5. Si**ya**hamba
6. Ndi**ya**phila
7. Si**ya**phila
8. Ndifunda ukuthetha isiXhosa
9. Sifunda ukuthetha isiXhosa
10. **U**thetha/**Ni**thetha kakuhle

Chapter Three

Exercise 1

1. Ewe, ndiyasebenza
2. Hayi, ndiyasala
3. Ewe, ndifunda isiXhosa
4. Hayi, sifuna ikofu
5. Ewe, siyaphila

Exercise 2

1. Uyaqonda?
2. Uhlala ekhaya?
3. Nifuna amanzi?
4. Uyagula?
5. Uyasebenza?
6. Nigoduka namhlanje?
7. Uyaphila?
8. Niyahamba ngoku?
9. Uyavuya?
10. Uthetha isiXhosa?

Ewe, ndiyaqonda
Ewe, ndihlala ekhaya
Ewe, sifuna amanzi
Ewe, ndiyagula
Hayi, ndisafunda
Ewe, sigoduka namhlanje
Hayi, ndiyagula
Ewe, siyahamba ngoku
Ewe, ndiyavuya
Ewe, ndithetha kancinci

Exercise 3

1. Ndiphila kakuhle
2. Ndivela eKapa
3. Ndifuna iti
4. Ndifuna uSipho
5. Ndihamba ngoku
6. Siphila kakuhle
7. Siya eBhayi
8. Sifunda isiXhosa
9. Sibona uLlzo
10. Sihamba namhlanje

Exercise 4

1. Ufunda ntoni?
2. Nivela phi?
3. Ufuna bani?
4. Niphila njani?
5. Ubona ntoni?
6. Uya phi?
7. Ubona bani?
8. Nifuna ntoni?
9. Ugoduka nini?
10. Uhamba nini?

Exercise 5

1.	Ngubani igama lakho?	**Ng**uNomsa
2.	Ngubani ifani yakho?	**Ng**uMalunga
3.	Ungubani?	**Nding**uJohn Matthews
4.	Ngubani ixesha?	**Ng**u11.15
5.	Uvela phi?	Ndivela eBhayi
6.	Uhlala phi?	Ndihlala eNew Brighton
7.	Uyasebenza?	Ewe, ndiyasebenza
8.	Usebenza phi?	Ndisebenza eKapa
9.	Uthetha isiNgesi?	Hayi, ndithetha isiXhosa
10.	Ufuna ntoni?	Ndifuna umsebenzi

Chapter Four

Umsebenzi 1

1.	umoya	Today there is wind
2.	ixesha	What is the time?
3.	isigama	Learn the vocabulary well!
4.	eMzantsi Afrika	We live in South Africa
5.	isiSuthu	Do you (pl) understand Sotho?
6.	Igama	My name is Mary
7.	amatikiti	I am buying tickets today
8.	umsebenzi	Do you want work?
9.	amanzi	We want water
10.	isipho	I want to buy a gift

Umsebenzi 2

The students are learning Xhosa. They are learning well.
John says: 'I like speaking Xhosa'
Mary says: 'I like speaking Xhosa too'
John and the others say: 'We are learning! We are glad!'
Mr Mhlaba, the teacher, says: 'Students, you are working nicely.'

Umsebenzi 3

a) Verb link = **u-**
1. The person is talking
2. Mary buys stamps
3. The woman is working
4. The student learns Xhosa
5. Father helps brother

b) Verb link = **ba-**
1. The people are glad
2. Mary, and the others, are glad
3. The women work
4. The students understand well
5. Father, and the others, help the lady

Umsebenzi 4

1.	**u-**	The child is playing	He/she is playing nicely
2.	**ba-**	The children help	They help (their) parents
3.	**u-**	Grandmother is sick	She is very sick
4.	**ba-**	Brother & co. are going	They are going now
5.	**u-**	Lumkile is drinking	He is drinking Fanta
6.	**ba-**	The parents are drinking	They are drinking tea
7.	**u-**	The young man is eating	He is eating bread
8.	**u-**	The teacher is talking	She is talking outside
9.	**ba-**	The gentlemen are working	They are working inside
10.	**u-**	The woman is buying	She is buying eggs

Umsebenzi 5

1. Abantu **ba**yahamba
2. Ugqirha **u**ncedisa abantu
3. Utata **u**phunga ikofu kodwa umama **u**phunga iti
4. Umntwana **u**thanda isidudu
5. UJohn **u**funda iphephandaba
6. Abafana **ba**funa umsebenzi
7. OoThandi **ba**yasebenza
8. Abantwana **ba**hlala ekhaya
9. USipho **u**hlala eKapa kodwa uThandi **u**hlala eBhayi
10. **Si**hlala eMzantsi Afrika

Umsebenzi 6

1.	**imi**buzo	3 & 4	question
2.	**izi**tulo	7 & 8	chair
3.	**ama**vili	5 & 6	wheel
4.	**imi**thetho	3 & 4	law
5.	**izi**fo	7 & 8	disease
6.	**ama**zwe	5 & 6	country
7.	**imi**thi	3 & 4	tree
8.	**ama**phephandaba	5 & 6	newspaper
9.	**izi**kolo	7 & 8	school
10	**imi**pu	3 & 4	gun

Umsebenzi 7

1. Umama uthenga **isonka**
2. UZola ugalela **amanzi**
3. Abantwana **ba**thanda ukutya **isidudu**
4. Umfundi ubuza **umbuzo**
5. OoThemba **ba**funda **iphephandaba**
6. Ipolisa **li**buza **imibuzo**
7. Umzali **u**funa **ugqirha**
8. Umoya **u**vuthuza kakhulu **eKapa**
9. Umsebenzi utshintsha **ivili**
10. Amawele **ah**leli **kamnandi**

Umsebenzi 8

1. Ewe, uyaphangela
2. Usebenza eKapa
3. Ewe, uthanda umsebenzi wakhe kakhulu
4. Uvuthuza gqitha!
5. Ewe, uyasebenza
6. Usebenza ekhaya
7. Ewe, bayafunda
8. Bafunda eVuyani, eGugulethu
9. Bancedisa abazali
10. Bahleli kamnandi

Chapter Five

Umsebenzi 1

1. Ncedani	Help
2. Hambani	Go
3. Sebenzani	Work
4. Godukani	Go home
5. Jongani	Look
6. Thulani	Be quiet
7. Vukani	Wake up
8. Phakamani	Get up
9. Mamelani	Listen
10. Phulaphulani	Pay attention

Umsebenzi 2

1. Ngena	Ngenani
2. Hlala phantsi	Hlalani phantsi
3. Hamba kakuhle	Hambani kakuhle
4. Sala kakuhle	Salani kakuhle
5. Galela amanzi	Galelani amanzi
6. Thenga isonka	Thengani isonka
7. Hlamba imoto	Hlambani imoto
8. Ncedisa umfazi	Ncedisani umfazi
9. Biza abantwana	Bizani abantwana
10. Jonga apha	Jongani apha

Umsebenzi 3

1. Jonga Nomsa
2. Vukani bantwana
3. Hamba kakuhle Themba
4. Salani kakuhle Lizo
5. Phulaphulani bafundi
6. Phakama mfana
7. Thulani bantwana
8. Mamela kakuhle mntwana
9. Hlala phantsi nkosikazi
10. Hlalani phantsi banumzana

Umsebenzi 4

1. **yi**tya
2. **yi**tyani
3. **yi**za
4. **yi**zani
5. **y**enza

Umsebenzi 5

1. hlala		6. **y**enza	
2. **yi**za		7. vala/vula	
3. sela		8. **yi**tya	
4. vula/vala		9. mamela	
5. funda		10. **yi**ya	

Umsebenzi 6

1. Musa ukuthetha	Musani ukuthetha
2. Musa ukujonga	Musani ukujonga
3. Musa ukudlala ...	Musani ukudlala ...
4. Musa ukuya ngoku	Musani ukuya ngoku
5. Musa ukuza ngomso	Musani ukuza ngomso

Umsebenzi 7

Singular

1. Thetha isiXhosa	Musa ukuthetha isiNgesi
2. Vala ifestile	Musa ukuvala ucango
3. Buza utata	Musa ukubuza umama
4. Biza ugqirha	Musa ukubiza uLizo
5. Yiza namhlanje	Musa ukuza ngomso

Plural

1. Thethani isiXhosa	Musani ukuthetha isiNgesi
2. Valani ifestile	Musani ukuvala ucango
3. Buzani utata	Musani ukubuza umama
4. Bizani ugqirha	Musani ukubiza uLizo
5. Yizani namhlanje	Musani ukuza ngomso

Umsebenzi 8

1. Musa ukulibala
2. Musa ukuxoka
3. Musa ukungxola
4. Musa ukuhleka
5. Musa ukulila

Umsebenzi 9

a)
1. Bancedisa abazali
2. Ufuna ukuhlamba imoto
3. Uncedisa utata
4. Basebenza ngaphandle
5. Ukhupha inkunkuma
6. Uyatshayela. Utshayela umgangatho
7. Uhlamba iimpahla
8. Bonke bayasebenza
9. Ewe, kulungile
10. Ewe, ndiyanceda. Ndihlamba izitya

b)
Umama ubiza abantwana. Kukho umsebenzi kakhulu namhlanje. Bayeza. UThemba uncedisa utata ngaphandle. Bahlamba imoto. UNomsa ukhupha inkunkuma. Emva koko utshayela umgangatho ekhitshini. Umama uhlamba iimpahla ngaphakathi. Bonke bayasebenza.

Umsebenzi 10

1. **ii**venkile   9 & 10
2. **ama**gama   5 & 6
3. **iin**cwadi   9 & 10
4. **ii**bhasi   9 & 10
5. **ama**polisa   5 & 6
6. **ii**kati   9 & 10
7. **izin**ja   9 & 10
8. **iim**puku   9 & 10
9. **ii**dolophu   9 & 10
10. **ama**thuba   5 & 6

Umsebenzi 11

1. incwadi   I am reading **a book**
2. ingozi   Beware of **danger** here
3. iifestile   Close **the windows**
4. into   Do you want **something** 'to' eat?
5. iti … ikofu   Do you want **tea** or **coffee?**
6. izindlu   People want **houses**
7. iindaba   Listen to **the news**
8. ipetroli   We buy **petrol** at the garage
9. inkunkuma   Take out **the rubbish**
10. izinto/iimpahla   Don't forget your **things/belongings**

Umsebenzi 12

1. i-   The bus is arriving
2. zi-   The cars are going
3. zi-   The girls answer the teacher
4. i-   The lady helps grandmother
5. zi-   The dogs see a cat
6. i-   The man is reading a book
7. a-   The girls are getting up
8. i-   The teacher asks questions
9. i-   The boy is playing
10. a-   The boys are playing

Umsebenzi 13

1. Indoda **i**hlamba **imoto**   The man washes **the car**
2. Iintombi **zi**thenga **iilekese**   The girls buy **sweets**
3. Inkwenkwe **i**vela **esikolweni**   The boy comes **from school**
4. Iinkomo **zi**sela **amanzi**   The cattle drink **water**
5. Intombazana **i**tshayela **umgangatho**   The girl sweeps **the floor**
6. Iibhasi **zi**hamba **ngomso**   The buses go **tomorrow**
7. Imoto **i**vela **eGoli**   The car comes **from Jo'burg**
8. Izinja **zi**luma **abantu**   Dogs bite **people**
9. Iikati **zi**thanda **iimpuku**   Cats like **mice**
10. Inkosikazi **i**cela **imali**   The lady asks for **money**

Umsebenzi 14

1. Ibulisa umakhulu
2. Ilesa incwadi
3. Ewe, kukho imifanekiso
4. Iyapeynta. Ipeynta indlu
5. Ibamba ileri. Incedisa utata
6. Ziyadlala
7. Iyapheka
8. Ipheka ekhitshini
9. Ewe, bonwabile
10. Ewe, ndonwabile

Umsebenzi 15

Inkwenkwe ilesa incwadi. Kukho imifanekiso encwadini. Umakhulu ubulisa inkwenkwe. Bajonga imifanekiso. Babona indoda. Ipeynta indlu. Inkwenkwe iyancedisa. Ibamba ileri. Iintombi ziyadlala. Inkosikazi iyapheka. Ipheka ekhitshini. Bonke bonwabile.

Umsebenzi 1

3 & 4	umzimba	imizimba	body	7 & 8	isifuba	izifuba	chest
9 & 10	intloko	iintloko	head	9 & 10	ingalo	iingalo	arm
14	ubuso	—	face	7 & 8	isandla	izandla	hand
11 & 10	(unwele)	iinwele	hair	3 & 4	umnwe	iminwe	finger
5 & 6	iliso	amehlo	eye	7 & 8	isisu	izisu	stomach
9 & 10	impumlo	iimpumlo	nose	9 & 10	(impundu)	iimpundu	buttocks
3 & 4	umlomo	imilomo	mouth	3 & 4	umlenze	imilenze	leg
5 & 6	izinyo	amazinyo	tooth	5 & 6	idolo	amadolo	knee
9 & 10	indlebe	iindlebe	ear	11 & 10	unyawo	iinyawo	foot
9 & 10	intamo	iintamo	neck	11 & 10	uzwane	iinzwane	toe
5 & 6	igxalaba	amagxa	shoulder				

Umsebenzi 2

1. librarian — 1a
2. shopkeeper — 1a
3. postman — 1a
4. milkman — 1a
5. taxi owner — 1a
6. mechanic — 1a
7. engineer — 9
8. judge — 9
9. nurse — 1
10. dentist — 1a

Umsebenzi 3

1. Danger
2. No dumping here
3. No entry
4. No smoking
5. Peace! Jobs! Freedom!
6. Private property
7. Entrance
8. Beware of the dog
9. Exit
10. Information

Chapter Six

Umsebenzi 1

1. ekhaya — Mother works **at** home
2. egaraji — Father buys petrol **at** the garage
3. efama — It is nice to live **on** a farm
4. eBhayi ... eKapa — The Ms come **from** PE but they live **in** CT now
5. Emini ... ebusuku — **In** the day we work but **at** night we sleep

Umsebenzi 2

1. Ndivela **e**Monti
2. Ndihlala **e**Goli
3. Ndiya **e**garaji
4. Ndivela **e**khemesti
5. Ndifunda **e**yunivesithi

Umsebenzi 3

1. kumakhulu — We have come **from** grandmother now
2. kooMadala — We are going **to** the Madalas tomorrow
3. kugqirha — The child is going **to** the doctor today
4. kuThixo — We ask for help **from** God
5. kunomathotholo — Dad likes to listen to the news **on** the radio

Umsebenzi 4

1. esonkeni — **on** the bread
2. evenkileni — **from** the shop
3. ebhankini — **to** the bank
4. emotweni — **in** the car
5. emsebenzini — **at** work
6. ephepheni — **on** the page
7. eposini — **in** the post
8. eketileni — **in** the kettle
9. esitulweni — **on** the chair
10. egumbini — **in** the room

Umsebenzi 5

1. encwadini — Write your name **in** the book!
2. etafileni — Mary puts the food **on** the table
3. edolophini — Father works **in** town
4. endleleni — I see a friend **on** the road
5. emvuleni — Don't walk **in** the rain!
6. elangeni — It is very hot **in** the sun today
7. ebhedini — The cat likes to sleep **on** the bed
8. entolongweni — There are many people **in** prison
9. emthini — Look at the birds **in** the tree!
10. ebhasini — The people climb **into** the bus

Umsebenzi 6

1. egaraji
2. ebhankini
3. eposini
4. ekhemesti
5. evenkileni

Umsebenzi 7

1. etini — Is there sugar **in** the tea?
2. eketileni — Is there water **in** the kettle?
3. esonkeni — Spread butter **on** the bread!
4. ekhitshini — Mother is working **in** the kitchen
5. esibhedlele — We visit a friend **at** the hospital
6. emotweni — Take the goods out of (**from**) the car!
7. kumabonakude — We listen to the news **on** television
8. kooSipho — Brother comes **from** Sipho and friends
9. endlwini — The children are playing **in** the house
10. eMzantsi Afrika — We need jobs **in** South Africa

Umsebenzi 8

1. Umama uthenga isonka **evenkileni**
2. Khupha ubisi **efrijini**
3. Amakhwenkwe ahlala **efama**
4. Amantombazana aya **kumakhulu** ngomso
5. Ubona ntoni **emfanekisweni**?
6. Ndiya **edolophini**
7. Utata usebenza **emini** kodwa **ebusuku** uyalala
8. Niya **kooSmith** ngomso?
9. Abantwana bafunda isiXhosa **esikolweni**
10. Lumkela iimoto **ezindleleni**

Umsebenzi 9

1. Baya edolophini
2. Ukhupha imoto egaraji
3. Bakhwela imoto
4. Uya eofisini
5. Uya ebhankini
6. Uya eposini
7. Ufuna ukuposa iileta nokuthenga izitampu
8. Bafuna iimpahla
9. Beware of cars on the roads
10. Ndidiniwe

Umsebenzi 10

OoMazibuko **ba**ya edolophini. Bakhwela **emotweni**. Utata uya **eofisini**. Umama uya ebhankini **kuqala**. Utsala **imali**. Emva koko uya **eposini**. Uposa **iileta**. Uthenga **izitampu**. Abantwana bafuna **iimpahla**. UThemba ufuna **ibhulukhwe** nehempe. UNomsa ufuna **ilokhwe** nezihlangu. Kamva **bayagoduka**. **Badiniwe**.

Umsebenzi 11

3 & 4	**um**nqwazi	**imi**nqwazi	hat	9 & 10	ibhatyi	iibhatyi	jacket
9 & 10	**ibhulukhwe**	iibhulukhwe	trousers	9 & 10	idyasi yemvula	iidyasi zemvula	raincoat
9 & 10	**ihempe**	iihempe	shirt	9 & 10	ikawusi	iikawusi	sock
9 & 10	**ilokhwe**	iilokhwe	dress	7 & 8	isihlangu	izihlangu	shoe
7 & 8	**isi**keti	**izi**keti	skirt	5 & 6	iqhina	ama**q**hina	tie
9 & 10	**ije**zi	**iije**zi	jersey	9 & 10	ibhanti	iibhanti	belt

Umsebenzi 12

1. It is cold **in winter** but it is hot **in summer**.
2. It is pleasant **in autumn** but the wind blows a lot **in spring**.
3. Schools close **in December and in** January.
4. **On** Monday, **on** Tuesday, **on** Wednesday, **on** Thursday **and on** Friday we work.
5. **On** Saturday we go to town. The children stay **at** home.
6. **On** Sunday we go to church.
7. The children study (go to school) **in the morning**. They play games **in the afternoon**.
8. Father arrives at home at 6.00 **in the evening**.
9. Excuse me. What **is** the time lady? It **is** 5.10.
10. I try to speak Xhosa **every day**!

Chapter Seven

Umsebenzi 1

1. **na**manzi	bread **and** water
2. **ne**bhotolo	bread **and** butter
3. **no**bisi	bread **and** milk
4. **na**bazali	child **and** parents
5. **ne**bhetri	oil **and** battery
6. **no**Themba	Nomsa **and** Themba
7. **na**nkwenkwe	girl **and** boy
8. **na**makhwenkwe	girls **and** boys
9. **no**mnqwazi	shoes **and** hat
10. **ne**siAfrikansi	Xhosa **and** Afrikaans

Umsebenzi 2

1. **noo**sisi	brothers **and** sisters
2. **nee**kati	dogs **and** cats
3. **nee**folokhwe	knives **and** forks
4. **noo**tata	mothers **and** fathers
5. **nee**kawusi	shoes **and** socks

Umsebenzi 3

1. ixesha **ne**mali
2. ibhanki **ne**posi
3. indoda **no**mfazi
4. amadoda **na**bafazi
5. umlilo **no**moya
6. ibhulukhwe **ne**hempe
7. ucango **nee**festile
8. iimela **na**macephe
9. ubhuti **noo**Sipho
10. imali **na**mandla

Umsebenzi 4

1.	**ba-**	Mother and father work
2.	**zi-**	The taxi and the bus arrive at 8.00 in the morning
3.	**zi-**	The dog and the cat sleep outside
4.	**ba-**	Men and women work on the farm
5.	**a-**	The boys and the girls are playing

Umsebenzi 5

1. Sifunda ukubhala **noku**thetha isiXhosa
2. Abantu bathanda ukutya **noku**sela
3. Abantwana bathanda ukudlala **noku**baleka
4. Ngempelaveki sithanda ukuphumla **noku**lala
5. Ndiyakwazi ukuthetha **noku**funda isiXhosa

Umsebenzi 6

1. **no**Thandi — I want to talk **to** Thandi
2. **na**bazali — The children go home **with** (their) parents
3. **ne**nja — The man walks on the mountain **with** the dog
4. **no**tata — Lizo works **with** father
5. **na**makhwenkwe — The girls play **with** the boys

Umsebenzi 7

1. Ndincokola **no**Jenny — I am chatting **to** Jenny
2. Uhlala **no**mhlobo — She stays **with** a friend
3. Badlala **na**bahlobo — They play **with** friends
4. Ndifuna ukuthetha **no**Nomsa — I want to speak **to** Nomsa
5. Usebenza **no**Themba noLizo — He works **with** Themba and Lizo

Umsebenzi 8

1. Ndi**no**mntwana — I **have** a child
2. Ndi**na**bantwana — I **have** children
3. Ndi**ne**nja — I **have** a dog
4. Ndi**ee**kati — I **have** cats
5. Ndi**no**msebenzi — I **have** a job
6. Ndi**ne**ndlu — I **have** a house
7. Ndi**na**bahlobo — I **have** friends
8. Ndi**ne**zitampu — I **have** stamps
9. Ndi**no**bisi — I **have** milk
10. Ndi**ne**phephandaba — I **have** a newspaper

Umsebenzi 9

1. U**no**msebenzi? — Ewe, ndi**no**msebenzi
2. U**ne**xesha? — Ewe, ndi**ne**xesha
3. U**na**matikiti? — Ewe, ndi**na**matikiti
4. U**no**mpu? — Ewe, ndi**no**mpu
5. U**ee**ncwadi? — Ewe, ndi**ee**ncwadi

Umsebenzi 10

1. Indoda i**ne**moto — The man **has** a car
2. UMary u**no**mntwana — Mary **has** a child
3. Iintombi zi**na**bahlobo — The girls **have** friends
4. Utata u**ne**fama — Father **has** a farm
5. Abamelwane ba**ne**zinja — The neighbours **have** dogs

Umsebenzi 11

1. Ewe, u**na**bazali — Yes, she **has** parents
2. Ewe, ba**ee**ncwadi — Yes, they **have** books
3. Ewe, i**no**msebenzi — Yes, he **has** a job
4. Ewe, ba**ne**zihlangu — Yes, they **have** shoes
5. Ewe, ndi**ne**bhatyi — Yes, I **have** a jacket

Umsebenzi 12

1. Ndi**ne**ntloko — I **have** a headache
2. U**ne**sifuba — He **has** a (bad) chest
3. I**no**mona — She **has** jealousy/is jealous
4. U**ne**sithuthuthu — He **has** a motorbike
5. U**ne**ngxaki — He **has** a problem

Umsebenzi 13

1. **na**bantwana — Parents **and** children are coming
2. **no**kubhala — I can speak **and** write Xhosa
3. **ne**ntombi — Sipho is talking **to** the girl
4. u**ne**ntloko — Nomsa **has** a headache
5. Ndi**ne**ngxaki — I **have** a problem

Umsebenzi 14

1. **nge**mela — We eat **with** a knife and fork
2. **nga**manzi — We wash **with** water and soap
3. **nge**moto — The young man goes **by** car
   ... **ngo**loliwe — or **by** train
4. **ngee**nyawo — The children go 'on' foot
5. **nge**sandla — The man 'holds' father **by** the hand

6. **nge**mali — We buy goods/clothes **with** money
7. **nge**pensile — Do you prefer to write **with** a penc|
   ... **ngo**siba — or **with** a pen?
8. **nge**zandla — Children like to eat **with** (their) har|
9. **nge**mela — Cut the bread **with** a knife
10. **nga**manzi — Fill the kettle **with** water

Umsebenzi 15

1. Uhamba **nge**sithuthuthu — He goes **by** motorbike
2. Baya **ngee**nyawo — They go on foot
3. Ubhatala **nge**tsheki — She pays **by** cheque
4. Ndibhala **ngo**siba — I am writing **with** a pen
5. Bathanda ukuhamba **ngee**teksi — They like to travel **by** taxi(s)

Umsebenzi 16

1. **ngo**tata — The woman asks **about** father
2. **nge**sikolo — Nono & co are talking **about** school
3. **nge**holide — Lindile writes **about** a holiday on the farm
4. **ngee**nyoka — The children learn **about** snakes at school
5. **nga**bafana — The girls chat **about** the young men

Umsebenzi 17

1. Ithetha **ngo**Lizo — He is talking **about** Lizo
2. Ubuza **nge**ngozi — He asks **about** the accident
3. **ngo**msebenzi — Tell me **about** your work
4. **ngo**ncedo — Thanks very much **for** the he|
5. **nge**mali — Thanks very much **for** the me|

180

Umsebenzi 18

1. Uya emsebenzini **nge**teksi
2. Uthanda ukuncokola **na**bantu
3. Bancokola **ngo**msebenzi, **nge**khaya **nanga**bahlobo
4. Ufunda isiNgesi emsebenzini
5. Bagoduka **ngo**5.30 ngokuhlwa
6. U**ne**sithuthuthu
7. Kuba siyakhawuleza
8. Bahamba **ngee**nyawo
9. Ewe/Hayi
10. Mna, ndihamba **nge**moto/**nge**teksi

Umsebenzi 19

1. **yena** Brother, **as for him**, he is laughing
2. **bona** The children, **as for them**, they are making noise
3. **yena** The child, **as for him**, he is lying
4. **bona** Mandisa & co, **as for them**, they ask for the key
5. **yona** The girl, **as for her**, she is crying
6. **zona** The girls, **as for them**, they are resting
7. **yona** The train, **as for it**, it is arriving
8. **zona** The trains, **as for them**, they are arriving late today
9. **yena** His father, **as for him**, he works in town
10. **bona** The neighbours, **as for them**, they are moving house

Umsebenzi 20

1. Wena
2. mna
3. yena
4. bona
5. nina
6. thina

Umsebenzi 21

1. Do you want to talk **to me**?
2. Yes, I want to talk **to you**
3. **I too**, am coming
4. **We too**, are well
5. We are talking **about him**
6. The letter comes **from them**
7. Do you have money? Yes, I **have (it)**
8. Do you (plural) have children? Yes, we **have (them)**
9. Are you going by aeroplane? Yes, I am going **'by it'**
10. **May** we meet **with you** (plural) tomorrow?

Umsebenzi 22

1. na**we**   I want to meet (with) **you** tomorrow
2. noyise   na**ye**   The child is similar to his father. He is similar to **him**
3. noMandisa   na**ye**   Lizo is getting married to Mandisa. He is getting married to **her**
4. nabahlobo   na**bo**   Thandi is meeting (with) friends. She is meeting (with) **them**
5. nonina   na**ye**   The girl is similar to her mother. She is similar to **her**

Umsebenzi 23

UThandi ubulisa abahlobo (bakhe). Bayancokola. Bancokola **nga**bantwana, **ngo**msebenzi, **nge**mali, njalo njalo. Uhlala phantsi **na**bo. Babuza imibuzo. UThandi uyaphendula. Uthi u**na**bantwana — inkwenkwe **ne**ntombi. Bona, bayafunda. Baya esikolweni **ngee**nyawo. UThandi, yena, uyafundisa. Uya emsebenzini **nge**teksi okanye **nge**bhasi. Umyeni (wakhe), yena, uhamba **nge**moto, kodwa ipetroli idulu. Abahlobo, **na**bo, bayakhalaza **nge**mali. Yonke into idulu namhlanje. S**inga**thini? UThandi uyagoduka kuba kuleythi. Abantwana babuya esikolweni **ngo**2. Uyabulisa.

Umsebenzi 24

1. Ufuna ukuthetha **no**Lizo
2. Hayi, akakho
3. Ubuya **ngo**2 emva kwemini
4. Ucela ukushiya umyalezo
5. Ewe, u**na**yo
6. Uthetha **ne**nkosikazi kaLizo
7. Ndi**nga**thetha **no**Vuyani?
8. Ngokuqinisekileyo
9. Ndithetha **na**bani?
10. Ndiyabulela

Chapter Eight

Umsebenzi 1

1. 11 & 10   **ii**ndonga   wall
2. 14   —   humanity
3. 15   —   speaking
4. 11 & 10   **izim**vo   opinion
5. 11   —   peace
6. 14   —   winter
7. 11 & 10   **iint**sapho   family
8. 15   —   death
9. 14   —   life
10. 11   **iin**gcango   door

Umsebenzi 2

1. **lu**dulu   Milk is expensive
2. **bu**dulu   Liquor is expensive
3. **ku**dulu   Food is expensive
4. **bu**yafika   Winter is arriving
5. **lu**fana   The baby resembles its mother
6. **Ku**njani?   How is it?
7. **Ku**lungile   It is fine
8. **Ku**mnandi   It is nice
9. **Ku**shushu   It is hot
10. **Ku**yabanda   It is cold

Umsebenzi 3

1. Ukutya **ku**dulu   Food is expensive
2. Ubisi **lu**shushu   The milk is hot
3. Ucango **lu**bomvu   The door is red
4. Ukuthetha **ku**nzima   Speaking is difficult
5. Ubusuku **bu**mnyama   The night is dark
6. Ulwandle **lu**blowu   The sea is blue
7. Ukubhala **ku**lula   Writing is easy
8. Ubomi **bu**nzima   Life is difficult
9. Uzwane **lu**buhlungu   The toe is painful
10. Ubushushu **bu**mnandi   The heat is nice

Umsebenzi 4

1. Usendlwini — She is in the house
2. Sisemotweni — It is in the car
3. Basemsebenzini — They are at work
4. Isesibhedlele — She is in hospital
5. Usekhitshini — She is in the kitchen
6. LisemaXhoseni — It is in (the land of) the Xhosas
7. Isentolongweni — He is in prison
8. Lusefrijini — It is in the fridge
9. Busetafileni — It is on the table
10. Kusekhabhathini — It is in the cupboard

Umsebenzi 5

1. Unjani umama? — How is mother?
2. Banjani ootata? — How are father and others?
3. Injani inkosikazi yakho? — How is your wife?
4. Unjani umyeni wakho? — How is your husband?
5. Banjani abantwana bakho? — How are your children?
6. Unjani umsebenzi wakho? — How is your work?
7. Sinjani isikolo? — How is school?
8. Linjani ibala? — What colour is it?
9. Injani impilo? — How is (your) health?
10. Bunjani ubomi — How is life?

Umsebenzi 6

1. UMary uphandle — Mary is outside
2. Izinja ziphakathi — The dogs are inside
3. Abantu baphambili — The people are in the front
4. Igadi isemva kwendlu — The garden is at the back of the house
5. Umthi usecaleni kwendlu — The tree is on the side of the house
6. Iimpahla zilapha — The goods are here
7. Isibane siphezulu — The light is above
8. Abamelwane bakhona — The neighbours are present/there
9. Amanzi alapho — The water is there
10. Isikolo siphaya — The school is over there

Umsebenzi 7

1. phantsi **ko**mthi — under the tree
2. phezu **kwe**khabhathi — on top of the cupboard
3. phambi **kwe**ndlu — in front of the house
4. emva **ko**cango — behind the door
5. ecaleni **ko**mlambo — on the side of the river
6. phakathi **kwa**maXhosa — among the Xhosas
7. phambi **ko**msebenzi — before work
8. emva **kwe**mini — after (mid)day
9. phambi **ko**kuhamba — before going
10. emva **ko**kutya — after eating

Umsebenzi 8

a)

1. Kuhle
2. Kumnandi
3. Kupholile
4. Kushushu
5. Kuyatshisa
6. Kuyana
7. Kubi
8. Kuyabanda
9. Kuyavuthuza
10. Kuyatshiza
11. Kuyaduduma
12. Kuyanetha

b)

1. kupholile
2. kuyabanda
3. kuyavuthuza
4. kushushu

Umsebenzi 9

1. Uhlala eKapa
2. Ubhalela uNomhle, umhlobo wakhe
3. Yena, useThekwini
4. Lihle, kushushu
5. Libi, kuyabanda
6. Uthi ufunda isiXhosa
7. Hayi, ufunda ebusuku qha
8. Hayi, kunzima
9. Ewe, ndifunda isiXhosa
10. Ewe, ndiyakwazi ... kancinci!

Umsebenzi 10

Game

1. soccer
2. rugby
3. cricket
4. tennis
5. hockey
6. golf
7. squash
8. athletics
9. swimming
10. boxing

Umsebenzi 11

1. Uthanda ukudlala igalufa?
2. Ukubaleka kumnandi
3. Amakhwenkwe namantombazana adlala ihoki
4. Sibukela irabhi nesoka ngempelaveki
5. Amakhwenkwe adlala iqakamba emabaleni esikolweni
6. Kumnandi ukudada xa kushushu
7. Umntu udlala isikwashi ngaphakathi
8. Sidlala intenetya ngoMgqibelo
9. Babukela umdlalo wamanqindi kumabonakude
10. Liphi ibala? Aphi amabala?

Chapter Nine

Umsebenzi 1

1. Hayi, **andi**hambi
2. Hayi, **andi**qondi
3. Hayi, **andi**fundi
4. Hayi, **asi**sebenzi
5. Hayi, **asi**goduki

Umsebenzi 2

1. **Andi**boni mntu — I do not see a person/anyone
2. **Asi**funi ti — We do not want tea
3. **Andi**thethi siJamani — I do not speak German
4. **Andi**funi lubisi — I do not want milk
5. **Asi**tyi nyama — I do not eat meat
6. **Andi**nxibi jezi — I am not wearing a jersey
7. **Asi**thandi zinyoka — We do not like snakes
8. **Asi**phumi ngokuhlwa — We are not going out in the evening
9. **Aku**qondi — You (sg) do not understand
10. **Ani**mameli — You (pl) do not listen

Umsebenzi 3

1. **aka**sebenzi
2. **aka**hambi
3. **aka**baleki
4. **aba**tyi
5. **aba**phangeli

Umsebenzi 5

1. Hayi, **andi**phangeli
2. Hayi, **asi**qondi
3. Hayi, **aka**guli
4. Hayi, **aba**guli
5. Hayi, **aka**nqeni
6. Hayi, **aba**nqeni
7. Hayi, **aba**celi cuba
8. Hayi, **aka**celi sigarethi
9. Hayi, **andi**tshayi
10. Hayi, **asi**tshayi

Umsebenzi 7

1. The wind is not blowing today
2. Trees do not grow in winter
3. The horse is not running
4. The men are not working today
5. The key does not go in/fit
6. The girl does not want to go
7. The dogs do not sleep inside
8. The baby does not cry
9. The winter does not end
10. The food does not burn

Umsebenzi 8

1. aka- awu- ayi-
2. weak .... vowel
3. strong ... consonant
4. a
5. i

Umsebenzi 10

1. akukho moya
2. akukho ndlela
3. akukho foni
4. akukho myalezo
5. akukho ngxaki
6. akakho
7. abakho
8. ayikho
9. akakho
10. azikho

Umsebenzi 13

1. Andi**sa**sebenzi kwaShell
2. Andi**ka**boni nto/mntu
3. UThemba aka**ka**gqibi
4. Ilanga ali**ka**phumi
5. Aku**sa**nethi/Aku**sa**ni

Umsebenzi 16

1. Ewe, ndiya**m**bona
2. Ewe, ndiya**ba**bona
3. Ewe, ndiya**yi**funa
4. Ewe, ndiya**zi**funa
5. Ewe, ndiya**yi**tya

Umsebenzi 4

1. Hayi, akasebenzi ngoMgqibelo
2. Hayi, naye akasebenzi ngoMgqibelo
3. Hayi, abasebenzi ngoMgqibelo
4. Hayi, akafuni
5. Uyanqena

Umsebenzi 6

1. **Andi**funi sonka
2. **Andi**funi ukuhamba
3. **Andi**sebenzi edolophini
4. Utata **aka**sebenzi ngempelaveki
5. Abantwana **aba**yi esikolweni namhlanje
6. UThemba **aka**thandi ukusebenza
7. Abafundi **aba**thandi ukufunda
8. Abantu **aba**tshayi kakhulu namhlanje
9. UThandi **aka**hlali ekhaya, uhlala eflethini
10. ULizo **aka**celi ukuhamba, uyahamba nje

Umsebenzi 9

1. **And**azi mpendulo
2. UThandi **ak**enzi nto namhlanje
3. OoMhlaba **ab**akhi ndlu
4. Intombi **ay**oyiki bumnyama
5. Abazali **aba**zi yonke into

I do not know an answer
Thandi is not doing anything today
The Mhlabas are not building a house
The girl is not afraid of darkness
Parents do not know everything

Umsebenzi 11

1. Hayi, andi**na**ntloko
2. Hayi, andi**na**bantwana
3. Hayi, asi**na**ngxaki
4. Hayi, asi**na**zinja
5. Hayi, aka**na**msebenzi
6. Hayi, ayi**na**zinkomo
7. Hayi, abana**na**zinto zokudlala
8. Hayi, aka**na**cuba
9. Hayi, azi**na**mali
10. Hayi, aka**na**foni

Umsebenzi 14

1. U**se**sibhedlele
2. Uthetha nogqirha
3. Hayi, akanantloko
4. Hayi, akakhohleli
5. Unendlebe
6. Hayi, akukho gazi endlebeni/igazi alikho endlebeni
7. Ufumana iyeza neepilisi
8. Hayi, akagoduki kwangoko, uya emsebenzini
9. Ku**se**buhlungu
10. Hayi, andinandlebe

Yes, I see **her**
Yes, I see **them**
Yes, I want **it/'one'**
Yes, I want **them/'some'**
Yes, I eat **it**

6. Baya ezivenkileni
7. Hayi, akanamali
8. Hayi, abadibani eposini. Badibana esitishini
9. Ngo10
10. Mna, ndihlamba imoto yam ngesiqhelo ngoMgqibelo

Umsebenzi 12

1. Andiqondi
2. UThemba akanqeni
3. Intombi ayinxibi jezi
4. Abantu abafuni ukusebenza
5. Andazi
6. Abantwana aboyiki zinja
7. Akubandi namhlanje
8. Akukho lubisi efrijini
9. Umama notata abakho
10. Asinamali

Umsebenzi 15

1. consonant .... k
2. verb link .... consonant
3. m .... verb link
4. w ..... u ..... a
5. y i

6. Ewe, ndiya**wa**tya
7. Ewe, ndiya**lu**sela
8. Ewe, ndiya**si**thetha
9. Ewe, ndiya**ku**thanda
10. Ewe, ndiya**ni**funa

Yes, I eat **them**
Yes, I drink **it**
Yes, I speak **it**
Yes, I love/like **you** (sg)
Yes, I want **you** (pl)

Umsebenzi 17

1. Ndincedisa umama	Ndiya**m**ncedisa
2. Sincedisa abahlobo	Siyaba**n**cedisa
3. Ndifunda isiXhosa	Ndiya**si**funda
4. Umfazi uhlamba iimpahla	Uya**zi**hlamba
5. Indoda ifuna umsebenzi	Iya**wu**funa
6. Umntwana usela ubisi	Uya**lu**sela
7. Abantwana basela amanzi	Baya**wa**sela
8. Umama uphunga iti	Uya**yi**phunga
9. Utata uthenga iphephandaba	Uya**li**thenga
10. UNomsa uthanda uThemba	Uya**m**thanda

Umsebenzi 18

1. Ndinga**ku**nceda?
2. Ndinga**ni**nceda?
3. Ndiyavuya uku**kw**azi
4. Ufunda isiXhosa? Ewe, ndiya**si**funda
5. Siya**yi**thenga indlu
6. Ndithanda uku**li**funda (iphephandaba) kusasa
7. U**yi**gcina phi? (ibhotolo)
8. Andi**wu**thandi umoya
9. Umntwana uyamoyika ugqirha
10. Uya**kw**azi ukuqhuba imoto?
11. Khawu**ndi**nike inamba yakho
12. Musa uku**yi**vala! (ifestile)

Umsebenzi 19

1. I see **myself** in the mirror
2. Do you work for **yourself**?
3. Mziwakhe works for **himself**
4. The children are hiding (**themselves**)
5. Do not worry (**yourself**)!

Umsebenzi 20

1. Uziva bhetele
2. Ewe, uthanda uku**si**funda
3. Hayi, akasafundi siXhosa
4. Aka**li**fumani ixesha
5. Ewe, uya**mazi**
6. Igama lakhe nguMnu. Mlambo/UnguMnu. Mlambo
7. Ucela ukubona incwadi kaKaren
8. Ufuna ukuthengela umhlobo wakhe, uBrian, incwadi
9. Umntu u**yi**thenga eCNA
10. Hayi, akanawotshi/akanayo
Hayi, andinawotshi/andinayo
Ewe, ndinewotshi/ndinayo

Umsebenzi 21

Nomhle and Karen are discussing (**it**) Xhosa.
Karen is studying **it**. Molly, as for her, she is no longer studying. She does not find (**it**) the time. Mr Mlambo is teaching **them**. Nomhle knows **him**, because he is a friend of Father. She remembers **him**. Karen says he teaches them well. Nomhle asks to see (**it**) her book. One gets (**it**) the book at CNA. It is only R100. It is cheap. Nomhle wants to buy it for her friend Brian. He too is trying to learn (**it**) Xhosa. Karen says she does not know (**it**) the time because she does not have a watch. Nevertheless, Nomhle goes. She says: 'Greet (**him**), Mr Mlambo!'

Chapter 10

Umsebenzi 1

1. **Ng**umntwana
2. **Ng**utata
3. **Ng**abantwana
4. **Ng**ootata
5. **Ng**umhlobo
6. **Ng**abahlobo
7. **Ng**umzekelo
8. **Ng**amakhwenkwe
9. **Ng**umXhosa
10. **Ng**amaXhosa

Umsebenzi 2

1. **Y**imoto
2. **Y**inkwenkwe
3. **Y**intombazana
4. **Y**imizekelo
5. **Y**imithetho
6. **Y**indoda
7. **Y**inkosikazi
8. **Y**ingozi
9. **Y**imilambo
10. **Y**imipu

Umsebenzi 3

1. **li**yeza	it is medicine
2. **lu**sana	it is a baby
3. **zi**zihlangu	they are shoes
4. **zi**intombi	they are girls
5. **si**sithuthu	it is a motorbike
6. **bu**busuku	it is night
7. **li**hashe	it is a horse
8. kukutya	it is food
9. **zi**zindlu	they are houses
10. **lu**sapho	it is a family

Umsebenzi 4

1. **ng**umfundi	it is a student
2. **ng**abafundi	they are students
3. **y**inyaniso	it is the truth
4. **li**thuba	it is an opportunity
5. **ng**uNomsa	it is Nomsa
6. **ng**oomama	it is mother and others
7. **lu**bisi	it is milk
8. **ng**umona	it is jealousy
9. **ng**amafutha	it is fat
10. **si**sifo	it is a disease

Umsebenzi 5

1. **Ng**uZola
2. **Ng**ooZola
3. **Y**inja
4. **Zi**zinja
5. **Ng**umntwana
6. **Ng**abantwana
7. **Si**sipho
8. **Zi**zipho
9. **Li**cici
10. **Ng**amacici

Umsebenzi 6

1. **Li**zulu nje!
2. **Y**imvula nje!
3. **Ng**umoya nje!
4. **Bu**bushushu nje!
5. **Y**ingqele nje!
6. **Ng**umsebenzi nje!
7. **Ng**abantwana nje!
8. **Bu**busika nje!
9. **Bu**budala nje!
10. **Bu**bomi nje!

Umsebenzi 7

1. UThemba **y**indoda — Themba is a man
2. UNothemba **ng**umfazi — Nothemba is a woman
3. Inkwenkwe **ng**uSipho — The boy is Sipho
4. Intombazana **ng**uSiphokazi — The girl is Siphokazi
5. Abantwana **ng**amakhwenkwe — The children are boys
6. Imoto **y**iToyota — The car is a Toyota
7. Ulwimi **s**isiXhosa — The language is Xhosa
8. Umfana **y**ititshala — The young man is a teacher
9. Utata **ng**unovenkile — Father is a shopkeeper
10. Ummelwane **ng**ugqirha — The neighbour is a doctor

Umsebenzi 8

1. umhlobo **w**akho — your friend
2. abahlobo **b**akho — your friends
3. igama **l**akho — your name
4. ifani **y**akho — your surname
5. izinto **z**akho — your things

Umsebenzi 9

1. umzimba **w**am
2. intloko **y**am
3. iliso **l**am
4. amehlo **a**m
5. iinwele **z**am
6. ubuso **b**akho
7. isifuba **s**akho
8. iminwe **y**akho
9. umlenze **w**akho
10. unyawo **lw**akho

Umsebenzi 10

1. **Ng**umhlobo *wam* — **It is** *my* friend
2. **Ng**abahlobo *bam* — **They are** *my* friends
3. **Ng**umyeni *wam* — **It is** *my* husband
4. **Y**inkosikazi *yam* — **It is** *my* wife
5. **Ng**umntwana *wam* — **It is** *my* child
6. **Ng**abantwana *bam* — **They are** *my* children
7. **Ng**unyana *wam* — **It is** *my* son
8. **Y**intombi *yam* — **It is** *my* daughter
9. **Ng**amawele *am* — **They are** *my* twins
10. **Ng**abazukulwana *bam* — **They are** *my* grandchildren

Umsebenzi 11

1. **I**phi imali **y**am? — **Nantsi!**
2. **Z**iphi iisigarethi **z**am? — **Nanzi!**
3. **S**iphi isitshixo **s**am? — **Nasi!**
4. **Z**iphi izitshixo **z**am? — **Nazi!**
5. **U**phi umntwana **w**am? — **Nanku!**
6. **B**aphi abantwana **b**akho? — **Naba!**
7. **L**iphi ikhaya **l**akho? — **Nali!**
8. **L**uphi usiba **lw**akho? — **Nalu!**
9. **U**phi umsebenzi **w**akho? — **Nangu!**
10. **A**phi amatikiti **a**kho? — **Nanga!**

Umsebenzi 12

1. **S**onke — We are **all** happy
2. **B**onke — **All** the people are happy
3. **Y**onke — **Every**thing is here
4. **z**onke — **All** the clothes are dirty
5. **o**nke — **All** the men are working
6. **y**onke — I am working **all** day/the **whole** day today
7. **W**onke — **Every** person likes kindness
8. **y**onke — Thandi works **every** day
9. **z**onke — **All** the schools close tomorrow
10. **b**onke — The dogs bark **all** night/the **whole** night

Umsebenzi 13

As for me, I am Themba Majola. I am a shopkeeper. I am married.
We live in Gugulethu, in Cape Town. We have children. 'They are' three. They are boys and a girl. They are still studying at school.
My parents are old. As for them, they live in East London.

Themba takes out photographs.

Here is my wife, Noluthando. As for her, she is a teacher.
Here are my children. This is Vusumzi, this is Mandla, this is Nontombi.
Here are my parents. Here is (my) mother, here is (my) father.
Here is the cat, here are the dogs.
As for us, we are all happy here at home!

Umsebenzi 14

1. I am well
2. Everything is fine
3. The wind is cool
4. The man is very fat
5. The boy is thin
6. The bread is finished
7. Are you (pl) hungry?
8. Education is very important
9. Are you married?
10. The shirt is clean
11. The washing is dry
12. We are all happy
13. The baby is tired
14. The dog is thirsty
15. I am 'full'!
16. The people are sitting on the grass
17. The children are asleep
18. Fana is right
19. It is cool in the shade
20. It is important to know (it) Xhosa

Umsebenzi 15

1. Ndiyatyeba
2. Uyabhitya
3. Iswekile iyaphela
4. Abantu bayalamba
5. Uyadinwa?
6. Ndityebile
7. Ubhityile
8. Iswekile iphelile
9. Abantu balambile
10. Udiniwe?

Umsebenzi 16

1. ibhasi
2. abazali
3. abantwana
4. ngomso
5. uSpar
6. inkosikazi
7. amapolisa
8. ubugqirha
9. uLizo
10. emanzini

Umsebenzi 17

1. Themba wants to sell his car
2. Raise (your) hand if you agree!
3. It is difficult to raise children
4. The sun is burning/is very hot today
5. Do you use a pencil or a pen?
6. Show me your work!
7. Boil water!
8. We feed the cats and the dog in the evening
9. Mr Mlambo teaches Xhosa
10. Bring your clothes/belongings!

Umsebenzi 18

1. Usually we see one another at church on Sunday
2. The workers greet each other in the morning
3. Themba and Nomsa understand each other
4. My children love one another
5. It is important to help each other

Umsebenzi 19

1. usebenz**ela** — Brother works **for** Mr Taliwe
2. bayancedis**ana** — Friends help **one another**
3. ubon**isa** — Father **shows** the traveller the way
4. bayathand**ana** — The girl and young man love **each other**
5. babuy**ela** — The children return **to** school tomorrow
6. ilind**ela** — **For** whom is the man waiting?
7. ubil**isa** — Mother **boils** water in the kettle
8. ubhal**ela** — Mary writes a letter **to** (her) parents
9. utheng**isa** — Mr Mbiza **sells** cars
10. utheng**ela** — The woman buys gifts **for** the children

Umsebenzi 20

1. Badibana eofisini kaNkosk. Zuma
2. Wenza isicelo somsebenzi
3. Ungunobhala
4. Ufuna ukubuza imibuzo
5. Hayi, akasebenzi
6. Ewe, unabantwana. Bathathu
7. Ewe, uyakwazi
8. Babhatala iR6000 ngenyanga
9. Ewe, uya**wu**fumana
10. Ungena **ngo**8 kusasa

Vocabulary

Nouns

| Verbs | p. 191 |
| General | p. 194 |

Noun Classes	Singular	Plural
1 & 2	um-	aba-
1a & 2a	u-	oo-
3 & 4	um-	imi-
5 & 6	ili-/i-	ama-
7 & 8	isi-	izi-
9 & 10	i-	ii-
	in-	iin-/izin-
	im-	iim-
11 & 10	ulu-	izin-/izim-
	u-	iin-/iim-
14	ubu-	–
15	uku-	–

A

accident	ingozi (iin-)
account	iakhawunti (ii-)
aeroplane	inqwelomoya (iin-)
Afrikaans	isiAfrikansi/isiBhulu
age	ubudala
answer	impendulo (iim-)
application	isicelo (izi-)
arm	ingalo (iin-)
autumn	ukwindla

B

baboon	imfene (iim-)
baby	usana (iintsana)
ball	ibhola (ii-)
bank	ibhanki (ii-)
battery	ibhetri (ii-)
beauty	ubuhle
bed	ibhedi (ii-)
beer	utywala
belongings	impahla (iim-)
belt	ibhanti (ii-)
bicycle	ibhayisekile (ii-)
bird	intaka (iin-)
blackness	ubumnyama
blood	igazi
body	umzimba (imi-)
bonnet	ibhonethi (ii-)
book	incwadi (iin-)
boy	inkwenkwe (amakhwenkwe)
bread	isonka
brick	isitena (izi-)
brother	ubhuti (oo-)
bus	ibhasi (ii-)
butter	ibhotolo
buttock/s	(im-) iimpundu

C

cake	ikeki (ii-)
car	imoto (ii-)
card	ikhadi (ama-)
cash	ikheshi
cat	ikati (ii-)
cattle (pl)	iinkomo
cattle kraal	ubuhlanti
chair	isitulo (izi-)
chance	ithuba (ama-)
character	isimilo (izi-)
chemist	ikhemesti (ii-)
cheque	itsheki (ii-)
chest	isifuba (izi-)
chief/lord	inkosi (iin-)
child	umntwana (aba-)

childhood	ubuntwana
Christmas	iKrismesi
church	icawa (ii-)
cigarette	isigarethi (ii-)
city	isixeko (izi-)
clan name	isiduko (izi-)
clothes	impahla (iim-)
cloud	ilifu (ama-)
coffee	ikofu
cold (a/the)	ingqele
colour	ibala (ama-)
	umbala (imi-)
community	uluntu
computer	ikhompyutha (ii-)
conversation	incoko (iin-)
country	ilizwe (ama-)
cow/bull/ox	inkomo (iin-)
cupboard	ikhabhathi (ii-)

D

danger	ingozi (iin-)
darling	isithandwa (izi-)
daughter	intombi (iin-)
day	imini (ii-)
day/date	umhla (imi-)
day (24 hr)	usuku (iintsuku)
death	ukufa
disease	isifo (izi-)
dish	isitya (izi-)
diviner	igqirha (ama-)
doctor	ugqirha (oo-)
dog	inja (izin-)
door	ucango (iingcango)
doorway	umnyango (imi-)
dress	ilokhwe (ii-)
duck	idada (ama-)
dust	uthuli

E

| ear | indlebe (iin-) |
| earring | icici (ama-) |

187

Easter	iPasika	homestead	umzi (imi-)
education	imfundo	honey	ubusi
egg	iqanda (ama-)	hope	ithemba (ama-)
elephant	indlovu (iin-)	horn	uphondo (iimpondo)
English	isiNgesi	horse	ihashe (ama-)
examination	uviwo (iim-)	hospital	isibhedlele (izi-)
example	umzekelo (imi-)	hour	iyure (ii-)
exercise	umsebenzi (imi-)	house	indlu (izin-)
eye	iliso (amehlo	humanity	ubuntu
		humility	intobeko
		husband	umyeni (aba-)
F		hymn	iculo (ama-)
face	ubuso		
family	usapho (iintsapho)		
farm	ifama (ii-)	**J**	
fat/oil	amafutha	jacket	ibhatyi (ii-)
father	utata/ubawo (oo-)	jealousy	umona
father (his/her)	uyise (oo-)	jersey	ijezi (ii-)
fever	ifiva	joy	uvuyo
field (sports)	ibala (ama-)	joyfulness	umvuyo
finger	umnwe (imi-)		
fire	umlilo (imi-)	**K**	
fish	intlanzi (iin-)	kettle	iketile (ii-)
flat	iflethi (ii-)	key	isitshixo (izi-)
floor	umgangatho (imi-)	kindness	ububele
food	ukutya	kitchen	ikhitshi (ama-)
foot	unyawo (iin-)	knee	idolo (ama-)
forest	ihlathi (ama-)	knife	imela (ii-)
fork	ifolokhwe (ii-)		
freedom	inkululeko	**L**	
fridge	ifriji (ii-)	ladder	ileri (ii-)
friend	umhlobo (aba-)	lady	inkosikazi (amakhosikazi)
friendship	ubuhlobo	land/soil	umhlaba
frog	isele (ama-)	language	ulwimi (ii-)
		law	umthetho (imi-)
G		leg	umlenze (imi-)
game	umdlalo (imi-)	lesson	isifundo (izi-)
garage	igaraji (ii-)	letter	ileta (ii-)
gentleman	umnumzana (aba-)	letter	incwadi (iin-)
German	isiJamani	life	ubomi
gift	isipho (izi-)	light	isibane (izi-)
girl (little)	intombazana	liquor	utywala
	(amantombazana)	love	uthando
girl (young)	intombi (iin-)	love of a mother	umsa
God	uThixo	luck/fortune	ithamsanqa (ama-)
grandchild	umzukulwana (aba-)		
grandfather	utatomkhulu (oo-)	**M**	
grandmother	umakhulu (oo-)	man	indoda (ama-)
grass	ingca	matter/affair	indaba (iin-)
greeting	umbuliso (imi-)	meat	inyama (iin-)
gun	umpu (imi-)	medicine	iyeza (ama-)
		medicine (profession)	ubugqirha
H		message	umyalezo (imi-)
habit	isiqhelo (izi-)	milk	ubisi
hair (animal)	uboya	minister (religious)	umfundisi (abe-)
hair (human)	(u-) iinwele	mirror	isipili (izi-)
hand	isandla (iz-)	misfortune	ilishwa (ama-)
hat	umnqwazi (imi-)	miss	inkosazana (amakhosazana)
head	intloko (iin-)	money	imali (ii-)
health	impilo	month/moon	inyanga (iin-)
heat	ubushushu	mother	umama (oo-)
help	uncedo	mother (his/her)	unina (oo-)
herbalist	ixhwele (ama-)	motorbike	isithuthuthu (izi-)
holiday	iholide (ii-)	mountain	intaba (iin-)
home	ikhaya (ama-)	mouse	impuku (iim-)

mouth	um**lomo (imi-)**
Mr	u**Mnumzana (oo-)**
Mrs	u**Nkosikazi (oo-)**
mud	u**daka**
music	um**culo**

N
name	i**gama (ama-)**
neck	in**tamo (iin-)**
neighbour	um**melwane (aba-)**
New Year	i**Nyibidyala**
news (pl)	ii**ndaba**
newspaper	i**phephandaba (ama-)**
night	ubu**suku**
nose	im**pumlo (iim-)**
number	i**namba (ii-)**

O
office	i**ofisi (ii-)**
oil	i**oyile**
opinion	ulu**vo (izimvo)**
opportunity	i**thuba (ama-)**

P
page/paper	i**phepha (ama-)**
parent	um**zali (aba-)**
parenthood	ubu**zali**
peace	u**xolo**
peel	i**xolo (ama-)**
pen	u**siba (iintsiba)**
pencil	i**pensile (ii-)**
person	um**ntu (aba-)**
petrol	i**petroli**
photograph	i**foto (ii-)**
picture	um**fanekiso (imi-)**
pill	i**pilisi (ii-)**
pipe	in**qawa (iin-)**
pity	u**sizi**
place	in**dawo (iin-)**
player	um**dlali (aba-)**
poem	um**hobe (imi-)**
poet (oral)	im**bongi (iim-)**
policeman	i**polisa (ama-)**
porridge	isi**dudu (izi-)**
post/p.office	i**posi (ii-)**
power/strength	ama**ndla**
prayer	um**thandazo (imi-)**
present/donation	i**lizo (ama-)**
prison/jail	in**tolongo (iin-)**
problem	in**gxaki (iin-)**
province	i**phondo (ama-)**
pump	im**pompo (iim-)**

Q
question	um**buzo (imi-)**

R
radio	u**nomathotholo (oo-)**
rain	im**vula (iim-)**
raincoat	i**dyasi yemvula** (**ii-** zemvula)
reference	i**referensi (ii-)**
request	isi**celo (izi-)**

river	um**lambo (imi-)**
road/way	in**dlela (iin-)**
room	i**gumbi (ama-)**
rubbish	in**kunkuma**

S
school	isi**kolo (izi-)**
sea	ul**wandle (ii-)**
secretary	u**nobhala (oo-)**
shade	um**thunzi (imi-)**
ship	in**qanawa (iin-)**
shirt	i**hempe (ii-)**
shoe	isi**hlangu (izi-)**
shop	i**venkile (ii-)**
shoulder	i**gxalaba (ama**gxa)
sister	u**sisi (oo-)**
skirt	isi**keti (izi-)**
snake	in**yoka (iin-)**
soap	i**sepha**
sock	i**kawusi (ii-)**
son	u**nyana (oo-)**
song	in**goma (iin-)**
Sotho	isi**Suthu**
sour milk	ama**si**
South Africa	u**M**zantsi Afrika
speaker	isi**thethi (izi-)**
speech	in**tetho (iin-)**
spoon	i**cephe (ama-)**
spring	in**tlakohlaza**
stamp	isi**tampu (izi-)**
station	isi**tishi (izi-)**
steam ship/train	isi**timela (Izl-)**
stick	ulu**thi (izinti)**
stomach	isi**su (izi-)**
stone	i**litye (ama-)**
street	isi**talato (izi-)**
student	um**fundi (aba-)**
sugar	i**swekile**
summer	i**hlobo**
sun	i**langa (ama-)**
Supreme Being	u**Qamata**
surname	i**fani (ii-)**
sweet	i**lekese (ii-)**
sympathy	u**sizi**

T
table	i**tafile (ii-)**
tank	i**tanki (ii-)**
taxi	i**teksi (ii-)**
tea	i**ti**
teacher	u**titshala (oo-)**
teacher (female)	u**titshalakazi (oo-)**
telephone	i**foni (ii-)**
television set	um**abonakude (oo-)**
thanks	um**bulelo (imi-)**
thief	i**sela (ama-)**
thing	in**to (izin-)**
ticket	i**tikiti (ama-)**
tie	i**qhina (ama-)**
time	i**xesha (ama-)**
tobacco	i**cuba (ama-)**
toe	u**zwane (iin-)**
tongue	ul**wimi (ama-)**

tooth	izinyo (ama-)
torch	itotshi (ii-)
town	idolophu (ii-)
toy	into yokudlala (izinto z-)
train	uloliwe (oo-)
	itreyini (ii-)
traveller	umhambi (aba-)
tree	umthi (imi-)
trousers (pair)	ibhulukhwe (ii-)
truth	inyaniso (iin-)
twin	iwele (ama-)

U

| uncle (maternal) | umalume (oo-) |
| university | iyunivesithi (ii-) |

V

| vocabulary | isigama |

W

wall	udonga (iin-)
washing	ivasi
watch	iwotshi (ii-)
water	amanzi
weather	izulu/imozulu
wedding	umtshato (imi-)
week	iveki (ii-)
weekend	impelaveki (iim-)
wheel	ivili (ama-)
wife	inkosikazi (amakhosikazi)
wind/air	umoya (imi-)
window	ifestile (ii-)
winter	ubusika
woman	umfazi (aba-)
wool	uboya
word	ilizwi (ama-)
world/earth	umhlaba (imi-)
work/job	umsebenzi (imi-)
worker	umsebenzi (aba-)

X

| Xhosa | isiXhosa |
| Xhosa person | umXhosa (ama-) |

Y

year	umnyaka (imi-)
young man	umfana (aba-)
youth	ulutsha

Z

| Zulu | isiZulu |
| Zulu person | umZulu (ama-) |

For vocabulary on:	See pages:
• occupations	58
• interesting words	60
• months and days	73
• sports	116 & 117
• place names	166 & 167

Verbs

Although the following words are all **verbs** in **Xhosa**, some are **adjectives** in **English**
eg: cool, fat, thin, happy, tired.

A

add	-ongeza
afraid	-oyika
agree/sing	-vuma
alive (be)	-phila
answer	-phendula
arrest	-bamba
arrive	-fika
ask (a question)	-buza
ask for/request	-cela
asleep (be)	-lele

B

bark	-khonkotha
be/become	-ba
begin	-qala
beware of	-lumkela
bite	-luma
bless	-sikelela
blow	-vuthuza
boil	-bila
boil something	-bilisa
borrow	-boleka
bring	-zisa
bring up/rear	-khulisa
build	-akha
burn/**be** on fire	-tsha
burn/**set** on fire	-tshisa
busy (become)	-xakeka
busy (be)	-xakekile
buy	-thenga

C

call	-biza
carry/bear	-thwala
catch	-bamba
change	-tshintsha
chat	-ncokola
check/look at	-khangela
choose	-khetha
clean (become)	-coceka
clean (be)	-cocekile
close	-vala
cold (be) things	-banda
cold (be) people	-godola
come	-za
come from	-vela
come in	-ngena
complain	-khalaza
congratulate	-vuyisana na-
cook	-pheka
cool (become)	-phola
cool (be)	-pholile
cough	-khohlela

count	-bala
cry	-lila
cut	-sika

D

dance (modern)	-danisa
dance (traditional)	-xhentsa
disappear/sink	-tshona
discuss	-xoxa
do	-enza
drink (cold)	-sela
drink (hot)	-phunga
drive	-qhuba
drizzle (to)	-tshiza
dry (become)	-oma
dry (be)	-omile

E

eat	-tya

F

fat (become)	-tyeba
fat (be)	-tyebile
fear	-oyika
feed	-tyisa
feel	-va
fight	-lwa
fill	-zalisa
finish/end/complete	-gqiba
finish (come to an end)	-phela
finished (be)	-phelile
forget	-libala
'full' (become) } of food	-hlutha
'full' (be) }	-hluthi

G

get dressed	-nxiba
get on	-khwela
get up/stand up	-phakama
get/receive	-fumana
give	-nika/-pha
glad (be)	-vuya
go/walk/travel	-hamba
go to	-ya
go home	-goduka
go in	-ngena
go out	-phuma
good (become)	-lunga
good (be)	-lungile
grateful (be)	-bulela
greet	-bulisa
grow	-khula
grow something	-khulisa

H

happy (become)	-onwaba
happy (be)	-onwabile
hear	-va
help	-nceda
help/assist someone	-ncedisa
hide	-fihla
hold	-bamba
hungry (become)	-lamba

hungry (be)	-lambile
hurry (become hurried)	-ngxama
hurry (be in a)	-ngxamile
hurry (be quick)	-khawuleza
hurry up (do quickly)	-khawulezisa

I

important (become)	-baluleka
important (be)	-balulekile

J

joyful (be)	-jabula

K

keep	-gcina
knock	-nkqonkqoza
know	-azi

L

laugh (at)	-hleka
lazy (be)	-nqena
learn	-funda
leave behind	-shiya
lend	-boleka
lie/fib	-xoka
lie down	-lala
lift/raise	-phakamisa
like/love	-thanda
listen	-mamela/
	-phulaphula
live/stay	-hlala
look (at)	-jonga/
	-khangela
look after	-gcina
look for	-funa
loosen/undress	-khulula

M

make	-enza
make a noise	-ngxola
make known	-azisa
marry (get married)	-tshata + na-
marry (be married)	-tshatile
meet with	-dibana + na-
move house	-fuduka

N

need	-funa

O

open	-vula

P

paint	-peynta
pay	-hlawula/-bhatala
pay attention	-phulaphula
phone	-fona
play	-dlala
post	-posa
pour	-galela
prefer	-khetha
pull	-tsala
pump	-mpompa

put on	-beka
put out/extinguish	-cima

Q

quiet (be)	-thula

R

rain	-na/-netha
read	-funda
receive	-fumana
rejoice	-vuyisana
remember	-khumbula
remind	-khumbuza
repair/mend	-lungisa
repeat	-phinda
rest	-phumla
return from	-buya
return to	-buyela
ride	-khwela
right (become)	-lunga
right (be)	-lungile
run	-baleka

S

say	-thi
scarce (become)	-nqaba
scarce (be)	-nqabile
scream	-khala
seated (be)	-hleli
see	-bona
sell	-thengisa
sew	-thunga
show	-bonisa
sick (be)	-gula
similar to (be)	-fana + na-
sing	-cula
sing joyfully	-tsholoza
sit	-hlala
sleep	-lala
slow (be)	-zekelela
smoke	-tshaya
speak/talk	-thetha
speak the truth	-nyanisa
spread	-qaba
start	-qala
stay/remain	-sala
stay/live	-hlala
stop/stand	-ma
study/learn	-funda
sweep	-tshayela
swim	-dada/-qubha
switch off	-cima

T

take	-thatha
take out	-khupha
talk	-thetha
teach	-fundisa
tell	-xela
tell to	-xelela
thin (become)	-bhitya
thin (be)	-bhityile
thirsty (become)	-nxanwa

thirsty (be)	-nxaniwe
tired (become)	-dinwa
tired (be)	-diniwe
throw away	-lahla
thunder	-duduma
translate	-guqula
translate into	-guqulela
truthful/right (be)	-nyanisile
try/strive	-zama

U

understand	-qonda
use	-sebenzisa

V

visit	-tyelela

W

wait	-linda
wait for	-lindela
wake up	-vuka
wake someone	-vusa
want/need	-funa
wash	-hlamba
watch (admire)	-buka/-bukela
wear	-nxiba
well (be/become)	-phila
well (be in good health)	-philile
well (be in good condition)	-lungile
welcome/receive	-amkela
welcome (be)	-amkelekile
wipe	-sula
withdraw	-tsala
work	-sebenza
work (be employed)	-phangela
worry/annoy	-khathaza
write	-bhala
write to	-bhalela

General

Some English **adjectives** which one would expect to find under **general**, are in fact **(stative) verbs** in Xhosa and are thus included under **verbs** eg: cool, fat, thin, happy, tired.

A

above	(nga)phezulu
	phezu kwa-
addition (in)	ukongeza
after	emva kwa-
after that	emva koko
afterwards	kamva
afternoon *in the*	emva kwemini/emalanga
again	kwakhona
all	-onke
all right	kulungile
amongst	phakathi kwa-
at (the place of)	kwa-

B

bad	-bi (adjective)
beautiful	-hle (adjective)
because	kuba
before	(nga)phambili
	phambi kwa-
behind	(ngas)emva
	emva kwa-
below	(nga)phantsi
	phantsi kwa-
better	-bhetele/-bhetere
black	-mnyama
blue	-blowu
both (people)	-bobabini
brown	-ntsundu/-mdaka
but	kodwa
by means of	nga-
by the way	kanene
by the way (remember)	kaloku
by yourself	ngokwakho
bye-bye	bhabhayi

C

can	-nga-
cheap	-tshiphu
certainly	ngokuqinisekileyo

D

dark	-mnyama
day *in the*	emini
day *the whole*	imini yonke
difficult	-nzima
dirty	-mdaka
down	phantsi

E

easy	-lula
etc. etc.	njalo njalo

evening *in the*	ngokuhlwa
every	-onke
every day	yonke imihla
everything	yonke into
exactly	kanye
excessively	gqitha
expensive	-dulu/-duru

F

fast	ngamandla
firstly	kuqala
fortunately	ngethamsanqa
front *in*	(nga)phambili
front *in ... of*	phambi kwa-

G

gee!	awu!
gosh!	yho! yho!
good!	heke!
green	-luhlaza
grey	-ngwevu

H

heavy	-nzima
here	apha
holy	-ngcwele
hot	-shushu
how	njani
how many	-ngaphi (adjective)
how much (money)	-malini
hullo	molo/molweni (sg/pl)

I

if	ukuba
immediately	kwangoko
inside	(nga)phakathi
	phakathi kwa-

J

just	nje

K

knock! knock!	nkqo! nkqo!

L

late	leythi/kade
later	kamva
light (in weight)	-lula
like that	njalo
like this	nje
little *a*	kancinci
lot *a*	kakhulu/gqitha
luckily	ngethamsanqa

M

many	-ninzi (adjective)
may	-nga-
morning *in the*	kusasa
must	kufuneka ...e

N

nevertheless	noko
next to	ecaleni kwa-

nice	-mnandi	**T**	
nicely	kamnandi	thank you/thanks	enkosi
night *in the*	ebusuku	that	ukuba (conjunction)
no	hayi	then/and so	ke
now	ngoku	there	apho
		there is/are	kukho
O		three times	kathathu
old	-dala	today	namhlanje
once (one time)	kanye	tomorrow	ngomso
one day	ngenye imini	top *on*	phezulu
only	kuphela/qha	top *on ... of*	phezu kwa-
or	okanye	twice	kabini
outside	(nga)phandle		
over there	phaya	**U**	
		ugly	-bi (adjective)
P		under	phantsi kwa-
painful	-buhlungu	unfortunately	ngelishwa
perhaps	mhlawumbi	usually	ngesiqhelo
pleasant	-mnandi		
pleasantly	kamnandi	**V**	
please	nceda/khawu ...e	very	kakhulu
pregnant	-nzima	very much	kakhulu/gqitha
present *be*	-khona/-kho	**W**	
		well	kakuhle
Q		well done!	heke!
quickly	ngokukhawuleza	wet	-manzi
		what	ntoni/-ni
R		when	nini
red	-bomvu	when	xa (conjunction)
		where	phi
S		whereas	kanti
sad	-lusizi	white	-mhlophe
side *on the*	ecaleni	who/whom	bani
side *on the ... of*	ecaleni kwa-	whole	-onke
soon	kamsinya	why	kutheni/ngo(ku)ba
sore	-buhlungu		
sorry (apology)	uxolo	**Y**	
sorry (sadness)	-lusizi	yellow	-lubhelu
still	-sa- (verb)	yes	ewe
	-se- (non-verb)	yesterday	izolo
strongly	ngamandla		

BIBLIOGRAPHY

A.C. Jordan, *A Practical Course in Xhosa* (Longmans 1966)

B. Kirsch & S. Skorge, *Masithethe isiXhosa* (Cape Town 1990)

B.E.N. Mahlasela, *Some Xhosa Idioms and Expressions* (Rhodes African languages department 1982)

S.Z. Zotwana, *Xhosa in Context* (Perskor 1991)

ACKNOWLEDGEMENTS

The author and publishers wish to acknowledge, with thanks, permission given
to use the material cited below.

- Ravan Press, extract from *The House of Phalo* by JB Peires.
- Doctor Russell Kaschula, extract from his article entitled, "Power and the Poet in Contemporary Transkei".
- William Heinemann, extract from *The Mind of South Africa* by Allister Sparks.
- Professor Tim Couzens, extract from an article on *Nkosi Sikelel'* iAfrika printed in the *Sunday Times* 13/10/94.

Background of the South African National Anthem

Before South Africa's first democratic elections in 1994, there were two anthems – an official and an unofficial one. The official anthem was *Die Stem van Suid Afrika/The Call of South Africa*. The unofficial anthem, *Nkosi Sikelel' iAfrika*, was sung by the majority of the population. After 1994 these were combined into today's official anthem.

Professor Mzilikazi Khumalo, retired African languages professor from the University of the Witwatersrand (with his team), was given the task of shortening the long dual anthem, and making it acceptable to all South Africans. No mean task! Professor Khumalo said that the most challenging part was to find a link that would join or blend the two pieces of music. "The words 'South Africa . . . South Africa' manage to bridge the gap nicely. It also lends a patriotic flavour to it," he said.

The anthem has four verses in four languages (see opposite page). The first two verses, in **Xhosa/Zulu** and **Sotho**, represent the two major African language groups, *Nguni* and *Sotho*. These verses are spiritual in nature. The third verse, in **Afrikaans**, extols the beauty of our land, and the last verse, in **English**, calls on us to stand together as a nation.

The spirit of reconciliation is embodied in our beautiful National Anthem. Now it's up to you to master the words!

N O T E : See page 168 for the words and background of the hymn, *Nkosi Sikelel' iAfrika*.

When South Africa was chosen to host the 1995 Rugby World Cup Tournament there was a wonderful opportunity to bring together the nation in support of our team. Manager of the Springbok Rugby Team, Morné du Plessis, saw the need for the players to show a commitment to the singing of the National Anthem before each match. It was my privilege to teach the *Amabhokobhoko*, and there was a sincere and enthusiastic response from the players and management.

As an observer remarked, "It was clear they'd been practising more than just their drop kicks and passes!"

Each year, with new players joining the squad, there was a pre-season "anthem training". Their enthusiasm and on-going commitment to singing the National Anthem with pride demonstrates the unifying power of sport.

The South African National Anthem

Xhosa / Zulu

Nkosi sikelel' iAfrika	*Lord bless Africa*
Maluphakanyisw' uphondo lwayo	*Let her horn/'spirit' be raised*
Yizwa imithandazo yethu	*Hear our prayers*
Nkosi sikelela thina lusapho lwayo	*Lord bless us her family*

Sotho

Morena boloka setjhaba sa heso	*Lord save our nation*
O fedise dintwa le matshwenyeho	*Stop the wars and the suffering*
O se boloke, O se boloke, setjhaba sa heso	*Save it, save it, our nation*
Setjhaba sa South Afrika	*The nation of South Africa*
South Afrika	*South Africa . . . . . .*

Afrikaans

Uit die blou van onse hemel	*Out of our blue sky*
Uit die diepte van ons see	*Out of our deep sea*
Oor ons ewige gebergtes	*Over our everlasting mountains*
Waar die kranse antwoord gee	*Where the crags answer ......*

English

Sounds the call to come together
And united we shall stand
Let us live and strive for freedom
In South Africa our land

ON TAPE/CD

- The spirit of reconciliation is embodied in the National Anthem, which combines verses in four languages from two anthems.
- The words South Africa form a bridge between the two anthems.
- It is a national symbol, along with the Flag and the Coat of Arms.

Extra Vocabulary

Extra Vocabulary

Notes